My Real Garden

**By real people who love to
get their hands dirty**

Ann-Marie Powell X

Edited by

**Ann-Marie Powell
& Tamsin Westhorpe**

This book first published in the UK by
My Real Garden
The Old Tractor Shed, Heath Farm, Heath Road,
Petersfield, Hampshire,
GU31 4HT

ISBN: 978-1-5272-8299-5

Designed, printed and bound in the UK by
Orphans Press, Leominster

CONTENTS

How My Real Garden Grew

On occasion, beautiful things rise up from ugly situations, right when you least expect them. On 23 March 2020, I stood in my kitchen and wept as it was announced on the news that there was to be national lockdown across the UK. Like all of us, my world suddenly shrink-wrapped around me. I felt unimaginably adrift, fearing for my garden design business and my family's future – I felt suddenly, unequivocally alone. Looking for solace, I stepped out into my much-neglected garden, found myself a trowel and, as I had countless times before, put my trust in Mother Nature.

But as an extrovert, I needed company, like-minded conversation, a focus and something to keep me motivated. So I decided to go live on Instagram that lunchtime. And somehow, after my first real foray into the world of social media broadcasting, I just kept on going.

Each day at 12:30 fellow gardeners came to chat, share, laugh, cry and spur each other on. I had found my tribe in the @myrealgarden community and our mutual joy in plants, garden wildlife and the natural world quickly created a virtual but very real bond. Tips were shared alongside favourite plants, tools and ways to grow as we found innovative ways to garden when the garden centres were closed.

Suddenly I realised that together, we were growing hope.

As nature carried on delivering beauty, butterflies and bees regardless of the global pandemic, our community grew as energetically as our plants. The passion was infectious, but in a good way! Our gardens made every day less difficult to bear and together we were all learning each lunchtime, no matter the size, shape or situation of the garden one tended, or indeed whether someone had a garden at all. Positivity was breeding content in a new and exciting way, and I wondered how this shared experience could perhaps help others.

This gardening book contains the real stories of people who have opened their garden gates and are letting others in because they know how their gardens have helped them physically and spiritually to appreciate what they have. Through the pages of this book, they all want to share the intimacy and the joy, the colour, the laughter and the learning that gardens and gardening provides us.

So please, turn the page, and – (socially distanced, of course!) – meet the gardening friends that have got me through a tough year. I hope that their words, their tips, advice, photographs and stories delight you and inspire you as much as they have me. With their help, I believe anyone can grow sunshine and hope.

It really is a very special kind of magic.

Ann-Marie Powell,
RHS Chelsea Gold medal winning garden designer.

Sow calendula seeds direct outside in early summer with the children.

CHAPTER 01

Family Plots

One of the hardest-working spaces of all has to be the family garden.
When there are children in the mix, there's heaps of fun to be had
and adventures to discover, right there in the back garden...

#familyplots

Above: The flowers of *Daucas carota* attract pollinating insects to the garden. Ann-Marie adores the flowers of umbellifers as they offer that airy relaxed look, perfect for a family garden.

© Rachel Warne

Where My Real Garden got started

I rolled my sleeves up, stepped outside and embraced Mother Nature

@myrealgarden

Name: Ann-Marie Powell
Location: Hampshire, England

DESCRIBE YOUR GARDEN?

Split over two levels, my own little Eden is the place where I revel in getting my hands dirty. A large, east-facing green oak deck surrounded with plants floats around the house. There's a shady boardwalk in the side passage clothed with a plethora of pots, leading to an oversized garden table that I made from a great slab of oak. Purposefully oversized, there's always space for friends and family to join us for breakfast (or evening drinks), for sowing seed, and pots of plants. Moving down the open, board oak steps

leads you to a circular lawn, the perfect size for family swingball tournaments. My veg splodge, mini-meadow and north- and south-facing borders allow me plentiful growing opportunities. It's an eclectic space, and all are welcome, particularly Mother Nature – we grow plants perfect for pollinators, have a mini pond for birds and dragonflies and a tall hedge that provides habitat and food for wildlife.

DO YOU GARDEN ALONE?

Jules, my partner, is a gardener but, to be honest, although we do garden together, I relish taking on the lion's share of the work. That said, it's fab to have someone

to discuss ideas with – but even after a long discussion I still do what I thought I would in the first place. The fact that if it all goes wrong, there's no one to blame but myself has probably saved our relationship! If pressed, our two boys, who are 11 and 16, will get involved, but only now and then. I hope the gardening is filtering in somehow – time will tell.

WHAT WAS YOUR LOCKDOWN EXPERIENCE?

I'm a garden designer and I think people would be surprised at just how many hours I usually spend behind a desk at a computer. Life before lockdown was fast-paced and frenetic, making sure other people's gardens looked beautiful whilst neglecting my own. After having the builders in, my garden really did look an absolute state, and it was long overdue to do something about it.

When lockdown begun, scared for my business and frightened for my family, I did the only thing I knew would keep me going. I rolled my sleeves up, stepped outside and embraced Mother Nature.

WHY HAS YOUR GARDEN BEEN SO IMPORTANT OVER LOCKDOWN?

I can honestly say that my garden has saved me through lockdown. It's been my sanctuary, my headspace, my sanity and my

#familyplots

friend. If I hadn't decided to hit that 'go live' button on Instagram back in March, I don't think I would have got through 2020 in one piece. The experience has given me hope, made me accountable, and turned me back into a hands-on gardener again. I honestly think before lockdown, I had lost my gardening mojo; now I can't imagine being without that honest, tired feeling of happiness after a hard day's graft amongst my own plants and nature. I owe all this to the @myrealgarden community – virtual, but real and so alive.

WHAT IS YOUR BEST MEMORY OF YOUR OWN GARDEN?
There are so many. Almost as soon as I started gardening at the end of March magic began to happen – seeds germinated, veg grew, birds arrived, butterflies floated and bees buzzed. Warm sunshine saw us engage more as a family and the children collected herbs, scrumped peas, swung in the hammock and sat by the fire pit. And the more I did, the more there was

to do. This gave me purpose, always knowing that around the world our community was doing the same, side by side and in my thoughts. I had constant companionship without physically seeing people outside of my immediate family during those months. I will always remember this precious time.

WHAT GARDENING ADVICE WOULD YOU LIKE TO SHARE?
Sow seed. Be it annual flowers, perennial bloomers, a meadow or some veg, seeds are endlessly fascinating, wonderfully exciting and easier to sow and grow than you think. They say that sometimes big things arrive in small packages, but I never thought seed packets would bring mountains of hope and emotion, attract wildlife and give love.

SHARE THE QUIRKIEST THING YOU'VE DONE IN YOUR GARDEN DURING LOCKDOWN?
I think dancing around a swingball pretending it was a maypole on May Day, wearing a floral crown fashioned from rhododendron blooms to Terry

"My garden has saved me through lockdown. It's been my sanctuary, my headspace, my sanity and my friend."

> "Step into your garden every single day, no matter the weather, and breathe in."

Wogan singing 'The Floral Dance' and broadcasting it live to the world on Instagram was pretty out there. Jules said he'd never been prouder of me in his life (ahhh!).

WHAT IS THE ONE THING YOU DISCOVERED DURING LOCKDOWN THAT YOU WILL REPEAT?
Step into your garden every single day, no matter the weather, and breathe in.

WHAT PLANT WOULD YOU NOT BE WITHOUT IN YOUR GARDEN?
Big question. I think my *Amelanchier lamarckii* gives me an inordinate amount of pleasure all year round.

WHAT (OR WHO) HAS BEEN YOUR MOST UNEXPECTED LOCKDOWN GARDEN VISITOR?
Dave and Maureen the collared doves. They became regular visitors to our small wildlife pond and became my new best friends.

TELL US YOUR GREATEST GARDENING SUCCESS.
All my veg – there's such unbelievable joy in eating your own food grown from seed. It's a revelation to me after not growing any for so many years. I'm determined to grow more, despite being challenged for space.

Allium 'Purple Rain' is a show stopping bulb with huge purple globes of flower up to 15cm in diameter. Wonderful to add colour to the border, great as a cut flower, and adored by bees and butterflies too.

11

#familyplots

Growing hope

What our gardens mean to us

@patton_kate

Name: Katie Patton
Location: London

@roz_gardens

Name: Roz Vincent
Location: North East Derbyshire

Work, rest, and play

Neither myself nor my husband were furloughed, so were attempting to juggle working our usual jobs whilst looking after our two-year-old. I was so grateful to have both outdoor space and good weather for the majority of lockdown – we spent lots of time learning to catch a ball, looking for bugs and discovering textures in the garden (soft, hard, sharp, smooth etc). Fairly early in lockdown, I managed to buy some

play sand and turned an old Belfast sink into a sandpit – that kept my toddler amused long enough for me to get one or two jobs done.

My garden kept me sane during lockdown, and there is no way I can understate that. It gave me everything from being able to sit outside and refocus between endless Zoom meetings, to keeping the toddler entertained, to indulging in a mindless activity such as weeding that forced me to switch off the technology and stop obsessing about "the figures". My garden has become my sanctuary from everything that is happening in the outside world, and when I sit out there in the evening with a glass of something cold, everything feels right – not perfect, but "enough".

> "Attempting to juggle working our usual jobs whilst looking after our two-year-old was a challenge."

Home-schooling adventure

As lockdown started, home schooling began. I was not destined to be a teacher, especially not to my own children. We were extremely grateful to have space for the trampoline for the children to get some exercise as well as a change of scene. Once lunch was cooked (often whilst watching the 12:30pm @myrealgarden) and schooling was over I was always extremely grateful to have some time to myself in the garden. My gardening was somewhat limited by a broken bone in my foot that needed surgery, on hold due to Covid-19, but pottering around and relaxing on the garden sofa and listening to the birds provided a bit of sanity.

I'm currently exploring a career change. Having quit a career in TV New Events planning, I have been attending classes at Capel Manor College in Middlesex and volunteering at our local English Heritage property, Marble Hill. When lockdown started both of these things, which were just

The garden helped me sleep at night

I am a lawyer with a busy litigation practice and can only describe my feelings on hearing our courts were closing to all but dire emergencies as a state of shock. The shock waves continued to hit as our lockdown unfolded in mid-March, just as the frost was coming out of the ground. All of the fears and stresses drove me out into the garden to cut new beds in the sticky mud while the children played "Zombie Apocalypse" around me – working out their own worries by beating up filled yard waste bags with sticks.

Gardening was something I could do. The fresh air in my lungs proved to me I was healthy, the smells of the earth convinced me my senses hadn't vanished and the hard work made me able to sleep at night. The outdoors was good for everyone in a small house during lockdown. It was creative and future-looking when every day seemed uncertain and disastrous.

@smalltowngardening

Name: Kat Kinch
Location: Warkworth, Ontario, Canada

2 DAYS AGO

"I was not destined to be a teacher, especially not to my own children."

for me, fell away and suddenly I was spending a lot of time teaching the children and producing a seemingly endless supply of meals. The garden was somewhere I could escape to once 3:20pm came and quietly deadhead, sow seeds, plant out, take stock and indulge my passion... until tummies starting rumbling again for tea of course.

Together in nature

We've enhanced this beautiful space

Name: Gillian Murray
Location: Scottish Borders

2 DAYS AGO

DESCRIBE YOUR GARDEN

Our garden is part of nature and the great outdoors. We are so lucky to have a river at the bottom of our garden creating movement and interest all through the year – and on occasions the river runs over the garden. We are surrounded by trees and our garden is on different levels with shady, dry, damp and sun trap areas. We have a pond too from the old run-off from the mill that used to be here.

DO YOU GARDEN ALONE?

Head gardener is how my family would see me but really, it's a joint affair with my partner and then there are the children dashing in and out with help and inspiration. I love plants, love to garden. Everything is thought about in connection with the nature we share our space with. Enhancing a beautiful space is completely therapeutic and sitting back and watching the different moments of glory the garden revels in is where we want to be.

WHAT WAS YOUR LOCKDOWN EXPERIENCE?

We had the ability to hideout as a family in this glorious space that we are lucky to be looking after. The garden was a retreat from the fears the world was under. Like finding @myrealgarden, being outside meant release of the stresses that could take us under. We got to connect more closely with nature and find real interest in how amazing plant life and nature is. Modern life is fast. Lockdown meant connecting together in a way that had so many benefits and the best place to do it was in the garden.

WHAT IS YOUR BEST MEMORY OF YOUR OWN GARDEN?

Getting to see moment to moment how things develop and change. Having sand martins turn up and make the riverbank at the bottom of our garden their home has to be a highlight for me. Sharing those moments with my family has been priceless.

WHAT GARDENING ADVICE WOULD YOU LIKE TO SHARE?

Don't get too hung up on controlling the garden. Give yourself as much time to enjoy it as you can. Watch it and see what is happy where, then make your changes. Any plants that are really happy will give you so many new plants by seed, division, healthy cuttings.

SHARE THE QUIRKIEST THING YOU'VE DONE IN YOUR GARDEN DURING LOCKDOWN?

Night-time walks around the garden when there was a full moon that lit up everything, and the clear night skies. Magical memories were created.

WHAT PLANT WOULD YOU NOT BE WITHOUT IN YOUR GARDEN?

Two wild plants our garden couldn't be without are forget-me-nots (myosotis) and red campion (*Silene dioica*) they just give so much. Oh, and how could I forget our ferns? We love ferns.

WHAT IS THE ONE THING YOU DISCOVERED DURING LOCKDOWN THAT YOU WILL REPEAT?

Slow life down and make time to be together in nature.

"Everything is thought about in connection with the nature we share our space with."

The children were entertained by digging holes, planting, watering and chilling out on the lawn under the trees. On clear nights a walk around the garden in the moonlight rounded off a busy day.

#familyplots

Vicky with hair up and head down busy working in her purple, pink and white colour themed part of the garden. Right: Scented Daphne.

I've learnt to share the space

Making perfume, potions and memories

DESCRIBE YOUR GARDEN.

I live in the town centre of Hitchin in Hertfordshire and my east-facing garden is fairly small at 17m x 5m. The garden is on two levels; the lower level is fully paved with a border either side, one in full sun and the other in part shade. There are two large raised beds and a number of containers. The colour scheme in this part of the garden is purple, pink and white, and is probably quite cottagey. The upper level, which I like to call the sun deck (because this is where I drink my wine in the evening sun), is fully paved, and all the planting is in containers, including two large troughs that run most of the length of the fence. I've experimented with using more hot colours in this part of the garden this year which I've loved and will continue to add to. I have two young children, so the garden also incorporates a Wendy house, sandpit and various ride-on toys that I'm always trying to position discreetly behind bushes. It's a constant battle for space!

DO YOU GARDEN ALONE?

I usually tackle the garden by myself but if extra muscle is required, I call in my partner.

WHAT WAS YOUR LOCKDOWN EXPERIENCE?

I usually garden when I am alone, or at least when the children are occupied. However, I rarely had this opportunity during lockdown so had to try to garden with my children 'helping'. Although this slows everything down, we had the time, and we created many memories all being together in the garden. It has been beautiful to see them take an interest in everything – sowing seed, hunting slugs and snails or mixing up perfumes made from herbs and petals. There have been flowers decapitated, plants sat on and branches torn from trees, but I've learned to relax more and share the space I used to see as mine.

WHY HAS YOUR GARDEN BEEN SO IMPORTANT OVER LOCKDOWN?

Walking into my garden during lockdown seemed to represent an escape from the chaos and mayhem of the world, and the responsibility that seemed to lie inside the house; not to mention home schooling and potty training. In the garden, I was in control. I could lose myself and become consumed by the moment and all other thoughts or concerns would leave my mind. This offered great therapy and left me feeling positive and recharged.

WHAT IS YOUR BEST MEMORY?

Enjoying the amazing sunshine whilst sunbathing and hopping in and out of the paddling pool. It's probably one of the only memories I have of actually relaxing in the garden, as I'm constantly fiddling, pulling out a weed or deadheading!

WHAT IS YOUR FAVOURITE GARDENING HACK?

If you own a large decorative container, don't plant directly into it but find some plastic pots that slide just inside that you can pot up, then lift in and out and replace as the display fades. I use this hack directly outside my back door and have a new display waiting in the wings each season.

SHARE THE QUIRKIEST THING YOU'VE DONE IN YOUR GARDEN DURING LOCKDOWN.

My daughter and I built a fairy garden under some shrubs using empty flowerpots as houses, leftover decorative slate as stepping stones and lots of glitter and fairy lights.

#familyplots

"There have been flowers decapitated, plants sat on and branches torn from trees, but I've learned to relax more and share the space I used to see as mine."

WHAT HAVE YOU DISCOVERED DURING LOCKDOWN THAT YOU'LL REPEAT?
I've discovered so much by watching @myrealgarden but one thing I've learnt that I will repeat forever more is how to train and tie in climbers horizontally, so that they actually cover the whole fence or wall and don't just fall about the place.

WHAT IS YOUR TOP RECYCLING IDEA?
We re-used cushions from an old sofa to make sunbeds for lounging in the garden.

WHAT PLANT WOULD YOU NOT BE WITHOUT IN YOUR GARDEN?
Definitely *Daphne odora* 'Aureomarginata'. My absolute favourite scent, ever. When it comes into flower I snip stems for every room in the house.

TELL US YOUR GREATEST GARDENING SUCCESS DURING LOCKDOWN.
I've transformed the back room of our house into an indoor garden; bursting with houseplants, some of which I've propagated myself. This acts as an extension of our outdoor space and I'm also hoping to use it as a bit of a greenhouse when I start sowing again.

"Being South Asian I couldn't be without growing my Vietnamese coriander for stews."
Osmawani @zephyrrivu

"My crab apple gave me beautiful white blossom in spring and small fruits in summer."
Amy Parker @AimFireUK

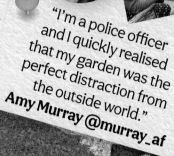

"I'm a police officer and I quickly realised that my garden was the perfect distraction from the outside world."
Amy Murray @murray_af

Sunny thoughts

"I love physical labour and being in nature. Gardening has given me a sense of purpose."
Lynn Shaw @melenesh

"On warm nights I loved staying out in the garden until late, watching the bats and listening to Motown music."
Julie Facey @jewelsofthegarden

"Cutting flowers to bring inside has been a joy."
Sue Hubbard @Hamstone_home

"Loved dipping my feet in the paddling pool and watching my daughter in our swing chair eating ice creams."
Claire Ling @choccoling

"We have views over the River Severn and have enjoyed the most amazing sunsets."
Jane Jefferies @dollybirdjj

Under an ancient oak

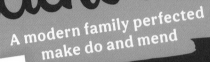

A modern family perfected make do and mend

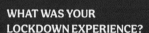

@sprout.up

Name: Seonaid Royall
Location: Brixton, London

2 DAYS AGO

have fires and relax. The curved beds are edged with raised weathered corten steel edging. This allows us to add a heavy mulch from our special homemade compost, which in turn allows us to grow a verdant array of shrubs and perennials. Near the back door is another patio where we probably get the best light, so it's where we do our pot vegetable gardening and sit to eat lunches in the dappled shade of the mature acer.

DO YOU GARDEN ALONE?
I'm a gardener so I garden with anyone that'll have me! Taught by my parents, it's now my livelihood. I work with a team of local women.

DESCRIBE YOUR GARDEN
It's a wonderful oasis under an ancient oak tree, which allowed us a full opportunity to create a stunning shady garden with separate entertaining and play areas. Lightening the canopy of the oak tree made it possible for a shade tolerant lawn to be a success. It's now home to a beautiful, handmade large swing. At the back of the garden is my office. In front of the office we catch the only sun possible on a circular patio, where we play darts,

WHAT WAS YOUR LOCKDOWN EXPERIENCE?
Our son got coronavirus early so we locked down before we were ready (no wine…). But being resilient we ransacked our booze cupboard, soldiered on, quickly embraced our urban oasis and turned it into our home school. We also did daily videos sharing gardening tips for families who were lucky enough to have a garden – or not. We sent out seeds and potatoes for other local families to grow and helped schools carry on gardening without my usual hands-on support. As lockdown carried on our huge oak came into leaf, so we gave it a lockdown haircut and made dens.

WHAT IS YOUR BEST MEMORY OF YOUR GARDEN?
Mine is an old memory. Just before we got married (in winter) we dug out the foundations for our garden room by hand, along with my parents and three brothers. It was brutal, it rained, I broke my ribs. But we did it.

WHAT IS YOUR FAVOURITE GARDENING ADVICE YOU'D LIKE TO SHARE?
If you like it, it's not a weed. If you don't like it, take it out.

Never a dull moment in this garden. They even opened a pizza restaurant on the shed roof and turned old tin cans into lanterns.

#familyplots

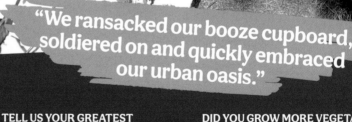

SHARE THE QUIRKIEST THING YOU'VE DONE IN YOUR GARDEN DURING LOCKDOWN.
The children set up a cafe that we could go to. This expanded to creating the next big Brixton eatery – a pizza restaurant on our shed roof. Even though we've had the garden room for 10 years we've never been on the roof, so opening night was VERY exciting...

WHAT IS THE ONE THING YOU DISCOVERED DURING LOCKDOWN THAT YOU WILL REPEAT?
Running as a family.

WHAT IS YOUR TOP UPCYCLING IDEA?
Over lockdown the children made tin telephones and then banged nails in them to make lanterns, just like I did as a child. They look lovely and took them hours.

WHAT PLANT WOULD YOU NOT BE WITHOUT IN YOUR GARDEN?
Our oak tree. It's everything to our garden, it's in constant use and view.

"We ransacked our booze cupboard, soldiered on and quickly embraced our urban oasis."

WHAT (OR WHO) HAS BEEN YOUR MOST UNEXPECTED LOCKDOWN GARDEN VISITOR?
The children built a bird box and were very surprised and thrilled to have a blue tit move in within a week of it being put in our tree. Unlike the butterfly feeders, that just look like tat hanging in the bushes.

TELL US YOUR GREATEST GARDENING SUCCESS DURING LOCKDOWN.
I took home the propagator from the school gardening club where they had planted some chilli seeds. After a few weeks they came up, the children potted them on and they grew into great plants.

DID YOU GROW MORE VEGETABLES DURING LOCKDOWN?
Yes. Just being around more meant I knew we could keep on top of feeding and watering. I only grew the things I knew we wanted to eat, potatoes, tomatoes, salad, runner beans.

You can be very creative by decking a small space. It's a place for picnics, drawing and playing but we've hidden a sandpit under ours too that we can transform into a paddling pool by filling it with water on a hot day.
Jenny Grainger @jennyudalegrainger

PRESCHOOL

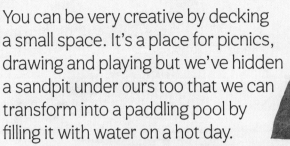

@moonlit_pebble

Claire Bickell
Go on a garden safari and hunt for mini beasts - watch them for a while in silence. Simple pleasures!

Hacks, Tips & Tricks

To take you from preschool to teens and beyond

One of the key elements of involving children in gardening is to play off their interests. So in my daughter Alice's case we've grown the fruit and veg she likes.
Joshua Johnson
@jobasha73

PRIMARY

@littlelifelovely

Charlotte Ward
Use your garden as a natural outdoor playground, an opportunity for your children to eat, play, plant, camp and stay up late and watch the stars. They really do grow as they grow!

Grow sunflowers together – a great way get your children into nature and away from the TV screen.
Amy Rose @amy_rosefletch

One of my best lockdown memories is being on the swings I hung from the pergola with my daughter Eva making up silly games to pass the time like 'Flip flop chip shot' – what a classic!
Peter Aylett @aylett_peter

Staying out late fire pit watching and dancing on the patio under the stars is a great way to get teenagers into the garden!
Chris Young @seewhygarden

A homemade tic-tac-toe game from an old slate and painted pebbles was a fun project for me and my daughter Sophie in our garden lockdown safe haven.
Samantha Wilson @samanthawilson3102

TEENS

Use wood shims and coloured permanent markers, sealing them to make them weather resistant, for vegetable markers. A great project to do with any age.
Leslie Macleod @belafieldgarden

@mypatchworkflowers

AND THE NEXT GENERATION...

Amanda Stothert
If you've space, keep ALL your garden toys, they hold so many memories! We have been here for 33 years, have four grown up children and now we can share our lovely space with our first grandchild.

CHAPTER 02

Cottage &
Country

A garden in a rural setting or with a traditional cottage garden look is something so many dream of. These gardeners have made it a reality by surrounding themselves with flowers, fruit and vegetables whilst embracing the views that lie beyond their boundaries.

The alliums and tulips of spring are replaced in summer by flowers that are great for cutting such as dahlias, sweet peas and ammi. There is a constant relay of flowers from spring until the first frosts of autumn.

A sense of purpose and pride

@smelaniesgarden

Name: Melanie Farrow
Location: Cheshire, England

#mygardenthismonth #weekendgardenparty
#gardengreatandsmall

DESCRIBE YOUR GARDEN.
My garden is a mixture of herbaceous borders with dots of formal box hedging to add structure. The beds are quite unruly and packed full of tulips and alliums in the spring, wildflowers in the summer and dahlia beds mixed with annual cosmos and ammi in late summer. There's also a greenhouse full of tomatoes, chillies and cucumbers, a cut flower bed and a ramshackle outhouse covered in wisteria. We have various seating areas and lots of old reclaimed pots bursting at the seams.

DO YOU GARDEN ALONE?
Mainly alone, yes, with help from the family occasionally.

WHAT WAS YOUR LOCKDOWN EXPERIENCE?
I was furloughed from work and suddenly found myself with so much time on my hands. Luckily, I had already filled my greenhouse with seedlings and the previous October we had doubled the size of every border, so I had a ready-made project to get on with. I became a full-time gardener overnight. I spent all day every day for about three months gardening. I absolutely loved it, and in May I won the #mygardenthismonth challenge on Instagram. It helped me to engage with and make so many friends from all over the world. It's been a truly amazing experience.

WHY WAS YOUR GARDEN SO IMPORTANT DURING LOCKDOWN?
It has been so good for my mental health being out there in all weathers, and getting my hands dirty has been fabulous. It's given me a real sense of purpose and pride. I have acquired so much knowledge – not just of gardening, nature and plants but I've learnt something about myself too. I am in my element when I'm out in the borders, deadheading or filling buckets with flowers to bring into the house to share with others.

WHAT IS YOUR BEST MEMORY OF YOUR GARDEN?
Just wandering around deadheading with a cup of tea or a glass of wine, admiring every tiny detail. Watching the sun move around the garden and seeing the beautiful sunset at the end of the day.

WHAT GARDENING HACK WOULD YOU LIKE TO SHARE?
Grow seeds – you'll save a small fortune. You don't need a greenhouse because you can grow biennials in late summer or put them on the windowsill in the spring. They are so easy to grow and so rewarding. Not to mention much more reasonable than buying plants.

SHARE THE QUIRKIEST THING YOU'VE DONE IN YOUR GARDEN DURING LOCKDOWN?
We had my dad's 80th birthday in the garden. There were just 6 of us with cake, Buck's Fizz and party games. I also held a reading group around the chimenea; we watched the sun set and the bats fly above us. (And as we hadn't seen each other for so long we had far too much to drink!) Plus my daughter celebrated the end of university exams in the paddling pool with a glass of champagne.

WHAT IS THE ONE THING YOU DISCOVERED DURING LOCKDOWN THAT YOU WILL REPEAT?
Sowing seeds for cut flowers. I've

"My daughter celebrated the end of university exams in the paddling pool with a glass of champagne!"

adored flower arranging with my own home-grown flowers.

WHAT IS YOUR TOP THRIFTY IDEA?
Using water butts and an underground well for watering my garden.

WHAT PLANT WOULD YOU NOT BE WITHOUT IN YOUR GARDEN?
Dahlias – I adore them. They are the most giving plants, so easy to grow, old-fashioned, so many varieties and colours and amazing for cut flowers.

WHAT (OR WHO) HAS BEEN YOUR MOST UNEXPECTED LOCKDOWN GARDEN VISITOR?
We have been inundated with bees. Like me they just couldn't resist the amazing number of flowers I had grown.

TELL US YOUR GREATEST GARDENING SUCCESS DURING LOCKDOWN.
Transforming a rockery into a bed next to the pond. I dug up the stones and planted a lot of seedlings in their place. It looks fabulous and has been a real talking point with the neighbours.

HAVE YOU GROWN MORE VEGETABLES DURING LOCKDOWN?
I have grown salad leaves, beans, tomatoes, chillies and cucumbers. The idea was to be more self-sufficient, but also they taste so much better than supermarket-bought veggies.

Growing hope

What my garden means to me

@Jane.louise.barker

Name: Jane Louise Barker
Location: Staffordshire, England

greenhouse space to cope! My seed-sowing adventure was a success. Thank heavens for the time granted by lockdown otherwise I'd never have got to work on time after mollycoddling all those tender plants in the mornings.

I am a veterinary nurse and was furloughed for a couple of months which was heart-breaking. However, I soon relished every day. I first tackled the front garden which had been a rockery by digging out enormous rocks and planting dahlias. I also created a border to grow my beloved lupin and delphinium seedlings to hopefully recreate the cottage garden border I used to love as a child.

Getting earth under my fingernails has been so healing and life changing. Gardening has given me a purpose and a wholeness that has offered a total escape. I'll never forget Mum's face when I picked her the first bunch of sweet peas that flowered. We were both moved to tears.

> **"I'll never forget Mum's face when I picked her the first bunch of sweet peas."**

Restoring the past

We have recently moved to live with my mum and renovate her country cottage. Lockdown was spent living onsite in caravans and restoring the beautiful garden that my lovely mum and wonderful late dad created throughout their married life. Sadly, dad suffered a severe stroke several years ago, which meant that the garden had been missing their tender loving care.

It is only in the last year that I have taken a keen interest in gardening and I went totally berserk trying to catch up on decades of missed knowledge. I was seed packet happy and had a go at growing everything I'd ever fancied, thinking that it would be a disaster. Result – not enough trays, pots or

The garden soothed me

@afroliage

...

Name: Marchelle
Location: Somerset, England

2 DAYS AGO

DESCRIBE YOUR GARDEN

We moved into this mature garden at the very end of 2019, when everything was winter dormant and still. It is under half an acre and the soil is heavy clay mixed with stony rubble. The site is a long, thin, steeply terraced slice of land surrounding our old country cottage, all bordered by hedging. There is a beech hedge along the road and a wonderful mixed native hedge backing onto fields. The sound of water echoes throughout thanks to a stream.

DO YOU GARDEN ALONE?

I am the head gardener, but it's very much a family garden, with my husband and children pitching in with great enthusiasm.

WHAT WAS YOUR LOCKDOWN EXPERIENCE?

Lockdown was a busy time for our family as my husband is a hospital consultant. I am also a doctor on a career break and so I was on reserve, but thankfully our area was spared high numbers of cases and my skills were not called upon. I spent my time home-schooling my young children in the garden, worrying about shielding grandparents and missing family overseas, from whom we were now indefinitely separated. A state of medical emergency is perhaps ultimately what you are trained for as a medic, but this was beyond anything we had ever imagined.

WHY WAS YOUR GARDEN SO IMPORTANT DURING LOCKDOWN?

Finding myself isolated in a new area, suddenly cut off from burgeoning friendships, with all the wider anxiety of a pandemic and personal anxiety of upheaval to our lives following our recent move was a very stressful time. Working in the garden soothed and grounded me like nothing else. I spent every spare moment out there and felt calmer, clearer and more resilient after every session. Gardening also kept me connected to the community as seeds and young plants were shared among neighbours. We felt very grateful to be locked down in such a beautiful and generous setting and community.

WHAT IS YOUR BEST MEMORY OF YOUR GARDEN?

Discovering beautiful plants already in existence here in the garden as they came to life in spring. This gave me such delight, especially the unexpected ones that reminded me of beloved gardens of my tropical childhood. Being able to share that enjoyment with my children has been my favourite memory of this season.

WHAT IS YOUR FAVOURITE GARDENING TIP YOU'D LIKE TO SHARE?

As a novice, my only tip is to just give things a go. I had never grown annuals from seed before, or planted out veg beds, but we gave it a go and had the joy of months of flowers, and delicious homegrown bounty. Also, mulch, mulch, mulch!

SHARE THE QUIRKIEST THING YOU'VE DONE IN YOUR GARDEN DURING LOCKDOWN?

We absolutely lived in the garden during lockdown, but we probably had the most fun sitting under the shrubs in the flower beds and paddling in the stream when the days got very hot.

Great fun was had paddling in the stream on hot days. Memories were created with and for the children which will remain precious for life. Being new to the garden there were constant surprises as the summer moved on.

#cottage&country

"Medical emergency is what you are trained for as a medic, but this was beyond anything we had ever imagined."

WHAT PLANT WOULD YOU NOT BE WITHOUT?
Wisteria. Living in a country cottage covered with wisteria has long been a dream, and now it is a dream come most deliciously true.

WHAT (OR WHO) WAS YOUR MOST UNEXPECTED LOCKDOWN GARDEN VISITOR?
I discovered a badger sett while weeding a flower bed, and also realised that bats had taken up residence in our loft. Those were the two most surprising wildlife discoveries of lockdown.

TELL US YOUR GREATEST GARDENING SUCCESS DURING LOCKDOWN.
Being able to draw inspiration, comfort, solace and beauty from the garden during what has been the most taxing time.

HAVE YOU GROWN MORE VEGETABLES DURING LOCKDOWN?
We grew many vegetables for the first time. I have long wanted my children to understand and appreciate where our food comes from, and lockdown provided the opportunity of time.

Name: Helier Bowling
Location: Hampshire, England

#weekendgardenparty
#mygardenthismonth

Little and often

Covid-19 knocked me back with tiredness – light gardening tasks were a blessing

DESCRIBE YOUR GARDEN
My garden is about an acre and is terraced on three levels. Near the house is a slate patio, outdoor sofa, table and two big flower beds, which are mainly planted in blue, purple and white. As you go up the garden path, the border gets a bit wilder, planted with grasses, late summer salvias and echinacea. At the top, through a rose arch, is my working garden. Here I have a cut flower garden of annuals that are all sown from seed, an ever-expanding dahlia bed, a vegetable patch, a few fruit trees, a wild garden area – and then there's my chickens. I adore cutting flowers from the garden to bring into the house. Some are sold to a few people locally and a nearby café. I have even done flowers for christenings and small weddings. My love for gardening has recently developed into designing borders and small gardens for other people.

DO YOU GARDEN ALONE?
I mainly garden alone, but my husband is keen and often helps with building things like raised beds and also tidying sheds (he's much better at that than me!) My boys used to do a little gardening but no longer. However, they do notice flowers and gardens, which I'm thrilled about.

WHAT WAS YOUR LOCKDOWN EXPERIENCE?
Lockdown coincided with me starting to sow my spring flower seeds. I spent days and days in the greenhouse, working through all my seeds. I had some old vegetable seeds that I was going to throw away, but when seeds started to be difficult to get hold of, I changed tack and sowed them too. My 2016 kale seed all germinated!

In March I caught Covid-19 and it knocked me back with tiredness. Being in my greenhouse doing a little light pricking out, whilst listening to the radio, was sometimes all I could manage. It taught me that gardening works well when you do little and often. I then decided to double the size of my flower cutting garden by digging out a bed that was taken over by ground elder. I did a little digging out every day and by the end of the week the ground elder was all gone. And then my plan was hatched to create a hazel arch for sweet peas and *Cobaea scandens* to scramble over… I'd always wanted to have one, having seen similar at Sarah Raven's garden.

WHY WAS YOUR GARDEN SO IMPORTANT DURING LOCKDOWN?
Every day I went into the garden to inspect progress. It became my new routine. I had a whole new set of Instagram gardening friends and we all spurred each other on. The hazel sweet pea arch started to take shape after years of saying I'd like one but never getting round to it. After the sweet pea arch came the second dahlia bed, the pergola, a water bowl, and now I'm planning a garden room/studio.

WHAT IS YOUR BEST MEMORY OF YOUR GARDEN?
Working in my garden while my 97-year old dad sat on the garden bench, watching me. My mother was unwell so he had come to stay with us for a few weeks. He would watch me plant out seedlings. I don't think he had quite realised just how much I love gardening before then.

WHAT IS YOUR FAVOURITE GARDENING HACK YOU'D LIKE TO SHARE?
Use what you have in the garden – I love keeping sticks for staking plants out and dried lavender cuttings are wonderful for kindling.

#cottage&country

"My teenage boys shaved their heads with clippers in the garden and styled their father's hair."

SHARE THE QUIRKIEST THING YOU'VE DONE IN YOUR GARDEN DURING LOCKDOWN.

My teenage boys shaved their heads with clippers in the garden and "styled" their father's hair when no one could go to the barbers. Also making a flower crown and filming a short "garden dancing" video and sharing it online.

WHAT IS YOUR TOP RECYCLING IDEA?

I staked my dahlias and cutting garden using a rusty metal concrete reinforcing grid from the builders' yard. The flowers grow through it and it supports them perfectly without having to tie them in.

WHAT PLANT WOULD YOU NOT BE WITHOUT IN YOUR GARDEN?

So difficult! Hellebores, alliums, cosmos, dahlias and agapanthus.

WHAT (OR WHO) HAS BEEN YOUR MOST UNEXPECTED LOCKDOWN GARDEN VISITOR?

So many birds, little robins wherever I've dug the soil.

Growing flowers for cutting in the garden is something I adore doing. Growing them from seed has saved me a fortune.

I have experienced an epiphany

The garden used to cause me anxiety but now it's my saviour

@jacquiecox

Name: Jacquie Cox
Location: Warwickshire, England

DESCRIBE YOUR GARDEN.
Our garden is approximately one acre. It was formerly part of a garden designed, planted and built by our parents for their property, Woodpeckers. It has a solid and mature structure that holds it all together but still gives a sense of endless possibilities. Following the division of the original garden there's still much work to be done – boundary plantings, new paths, parking and so on – while placing my own stamp on it without detracting from or eradicating what already exists.

The formal areas run parallel to a row of old stone farm workers' cottages, one of which I own, and include a (now rather neglected) rose garden surrounded by yew hedges; a potager enclosed by buxus (box) hedging and accessed by four apple arches, where vegetables, cut flowers and lavenders are grown; and lastly a knot garden with a topiary/gravel garden.

The informal areas comprise long and short grass areas under trees and a comfrey 'field', which lead to and surround a two-storey oak-framed building and include drifts of many different snowdrop cultivars, two new wildflower meadows, and a new tropical corner.

DO YOU GARDEN ALONE?
I am eternally grateful for any help I can get my hands on. I'm helped by two gardeners once a week for a half a day and my brothers will muck in when needed.

WHAT WAS YOUR LOCKDOWN EXPERIENCE?
From the moment I had to self-isolate, prior to official lockdown, I found contentment working from my newly renovated cottage. I adored my life in London, but I was definitely burning the candle at both ends and starting to feel the consequences. Taking my foot off the accelerator and allowing things to flow naturally was lifesaving and liberating. The garden I inherited that had previously caused some anxiety suddenly became my saviour.

WHY WAS YOUR GARDEN SO IMPORTANT DURING LOCKDOWN?
I have been told by family and friends that they feel I have experienced an epiphany. I agree – I've had a spectacular metamorphosis. The most important part for me is that I am so grateful every day that I have the privilege of a garden. The guilt that keeps me awake is that I am loving life while others have lost theirs; and for those who are suffering financially in this uncertain world; and for those who do not have access to green space.

WHAT IS YOUR BEST MEMORY OF YOUR GARDEN?
It's of our parents every time I step into what they created. They would be amazed I have been infected by the gardening bug. There is something reassuring and primeval about walking on the paths they laid and digging the borders they created. If only they could see me now!

WHAT IS YOUR FAVOURITE GARDENING TIP YOU'D LIKE TO SHARE?
Leave it to the experts – but when you cannot afford them, have confidence in your instincts.

Inheriting a garden leaves you the opportunity to continue its story and add another chapter all of your own. Classic cottage garden plants such as roses and agapanthus are prefect for this plot.

PITMASTON PINEAPPLE 1735

MARGIL (PROBABLY NORMAN)

STON PPIN 1709

#cottage&country

> "There is something primeval about walking on the paths they laid and digging the borders they created. If only they could see me now."

SHARE THE QUIRKIEST THING YOU'VE DONE IN YOUR GARDEN DURING LOCKDOWN.
The moment that we could invite family and friends back into our gardens – and every visitor since has made their own precious memory – we started with inviting a male neighbour to urinate daily in my wildflower meadow! It was an attempt to deter the lone badger who had chosen a prime spot for his latrine (but our cunning plan did not work).

WHAT IS THE ONE THING YOU DISCOVERED DURING LOCKDOWN THAT YOU WILL REPEAT?
Rain or shine I want and need to be in the garden morning and evening. I will continue to watch and learn from the universal gardening community.

WHAT IS YOUR TOP UPCYCLING IDEA?
I bury household breakages instead of sending them to landfill. I have an Archaeology degree, so when I come across old bottles or clay pipes, ironwork or crockery shards in the garden from previous centuries I get excited. It is quite possible that in 50 years' time a robot will bulldoze my garden and will try to make sense of the fragments.

WHAT PLANT WOULD YOU NOT BE WITHOUT IN YOUR GARDEN?
Sweet peas – for their amazing scent and proliferation, which enabled me to gift bunches of them to neighbours during lockdown.

WHAT (OR WHO) HAS BEEN YOUR MOST UNEXPECTED LOCKDOWN GARDEN VISITOR?
A dehydrated little newt on the threshold of my cottage in the first days of lockdown. I nursed it and expected I would find it dead in the morning but happily it escaped my temporary pond.

SHARE YOUR GREATEST GARDENING SUCCESS DURING LOCKDOWN.
Growing from seed for the first time; and feeling a bit more in control of weeds and the garden in general.

Growing hope

What my garden means to me

@imgood15

Name: Judi Mcintosh
Location: Petersfield, England

get rather lonely after a couple of weeks as I'm normally a very sociable person. My usual clubs, which include groups for cryptic crosswords, choir, art history and Spanish all suddenly stopped, as did going to the gym. Gradually, as things eased slightly, I was able to invite friends and neighbours around the side of the house for tea or drinkies at the bottom of the garden. We have an outside loo and with social distancing we could feel a sense of normality – and get slightly pie-eyed with impunity! The thought of visitors coming to the garden kept me from slacking on the gardening front as I was keen to impress them all with my perky and pretty plants.

> **"The thought of visitors coming to the garden kept me from slacking."**

Weeding took away the worry

At the beginning of lockdown, being over 70, I was made to feel quite concerned for my safety. All my four children were affected financially and in other ways by the threat of the virus. My youngest was expecting a baby and commuting to London, so I did worry about my children a lot. So I concentrated madly on my rather neglected garden. I bashed away at it, which was a positive way through the gloom and worry. My garden and I both benefited enormously from tuning to Ann-Marie's Live Instagram. The Sunday socials and daily chats were inspirational. I felt part of a community again. I did still

Right; My son's used the metal hoops from a rotten brandy barrel to make a garden feature and it is now a much prized possession

We made compost in just 4 months

The garden never stopped producing tasks - it just kept on giving

@61morganb

Name: Becca Morgan
Location: Wantage, Oxfordshire, England

2 DAYS AGO

DESCRIBE YOUR GARDEN

It's a country village garden of about half an acre. The house sits in the middle of the plot, so it feels smaller than that. In the 20 years we've lived here, it's changed from a playground to somewhere more gardened. To start with we just tried to tame it, as it was so overgrown, but slowly having removed lots of conifers we found that plants grew better, as they weren't being robbed of moisture, nutrients and light.

The garden is on a slope, with the principle rooms of the house looking up onto the main garden, which gives the house the feeling of facing an amphitheatre. I feel that the garden needs to perform and provide the "view" for the house. I like creating little spots of interest around the plot, to maybe stop and sit – which we hardly do!

We enjoy eating outside and using the garden in the evening, so we've installed lighting, which gives a whole other atmosphere.

DO YOU GARDEN ALONE?

I'm Head Gardener, it's my hobby and my challenge, but I do rely on my men for the mowing, hedge cutting and digging up stumps etc. However, they do all appreciate the finer details, even if they don't want to 'garden'.

WHAT WAS YOUR LOCKDOWN EXPERIENCE?

It allowed me more time for thought to challenge where and what things were planted – so it involved lots of lifting, dividing, replanting and re-jigging the borders. My boys are strong and fit and along with some extreme compost management, they rebuilt the log store, which now looks like something out of an alpine village. We're all chuffed with the achievement of growing seeds and set up a propagation table so we can do more in the future. The garden never stopped producing more tasks, and it never stopped giving.

WHY WAS YOUR GARDEN SO IMPORTANT DURING LOCKDOWN?

It's never felt more important to the family. Every night, eating supper outside, we repeated to ourselves how lucky we were to have this amazing space. The garden gave us shared purpose and goals, it kept us busy and focused.

WHAT IS YOUR BEST MEMORY OF YOUR OWN GARDEN?

Having the time to stop and notice things. Being here together and appreciating each fleeting moment. Just generally being more aware of the garden and nature.

WHAT IS YOUR FAVOURITE GARDENING TIP?

Set up a watering system for the raspberries. Ours comes on for 10 minutes in the morning and the same at night.

SHARE THE QUIRKIEST THING YOU'VE DONE IN YOUR GARDEN DURING LOCKDOWN?

The previously hardly used croquet set provided hours of fun as we made up new rules to cope with our sloping lawn. There were clear nights lying on the grass identifying the stars and once we spotted the International Space Station the day of the Space X launch.

WHAT HAVE YOU DISCOVERED DURING LOCKDOWN THAT YOU WILL REPEAT?

That we are capable of growing from seed. I've become a bit of an Instagram groupie, with

#cottage&country

> "The previously hardly used croquet set provided hours of fun as we made up new rules to cope with our sloping lawn."

@myrealgarden, which then led me on to other related accounts, and as a result my gardening knowledge has expanded.

WHAT IS YOUR TOP UPCYCLING IDEA?

Make a barrel sphere. My late father gave me a beautiful old wooden brandy barrel years ago, which I didn't look after, so it rotted. But having thrown away all the wood, I never got around to throwing out the metal hoops. Both my boys are engineers and they decided that this "junk" needed to be repurposed, so they made me a wonderful metal sphere. Now I have something to cherish that will remind me of both my dad and my sons.

WHAT PLANT WOULD YOU NOT BE WITHOUT IN YOUR GARDEN?

Yew. It divides our spaces. It gives year-round structure. It's tactile and forgiving. It can provide privacy and be made into topiary.

WHAT (OR WHO) HAS BEEN YOUR MOST UNEXPECTED LOCKDOWN GARDEN VISITOR?

We've too many pigeons, but we did notice more blackbirds and thrushes. We always enjoy the butterflies, dragonflies, bees and newts in and around the pond.

SHARE YOUR GREATEST GARDENING SUCCESS DURING LOCKDOWN.

We made compost as we couldn't go to the recycling centre. We recorded the temperature of the bins, turning the heaps every time they dipped. Everything was chopped and shredded and the result was a stunning compost within 4 months – rather than the year it normally takes.

HAVE YOU GROWN MORE VEGETABLES DURING LOCKDOWN?

I've bought lots of seeds over the years, but never found the time to actually sow anything. So in fact I didn't need to buy seed, I just needed to sow what I had already – and some of it actually worked!

My garden needed me, and I needed my garden

I'd rest in the hammock and make plans for the future of the garden

@lyndasunset

Name: Lynda Griffiths
Location: Wiltshire, England

#lovemygarden #lovetogarden
#perennialgardener #beautifulblooms

DESCRIBE YOUR GARDEN

My garden is a 1.2 acre plot that extends to the front and side of our 200-year-old cottage. The upper level is laid mainly to lawn, with several mature trees and shrubs, and surrounded by Cotswold stone walls. This is where I have my flower borders planted mainly with perennials, bulbs, shrubs and roses. There are several flowering cherry trees, which are an absolute delight in spring. The lower 'secret' garden is hidden from view until you follow a sloping track that opens out into a woodland glade. This is a wonderful shady area to sit and feel at one with nature. I have added to the borrowed landscape of the adjacent fields by planting woodland plants and shrubs. From here, you pass through a rose-covered gateway into an orchard and wild grass area.

DO YOU GARDEN ALONE?

I garden with my husband – he's my gofer! He'll chop, cut, strim, lift, carry and water but he hasn't a clue about plants and can't distinguish a weed from a prizewinner. He is therefore directed and watched carefully. Oh, and my son is always keen to wield the chainsaw when a tree needs felling.

WHAT WAS YOUR LOCKDOWN EXPERIENCE?

My garden was my safe place and sanctuary in lockdown, as I was in the vulnerable category that had to 'shield'. That meant I was confined to home for three months and could not go anywhere at all. The last couple of years have been difficult for my garden. Being a full-time teacher meant it usually only received a cursory trim and prune at weekends. Then I was diagnosed with blood cancer and my garden was totally neglected while I started my treatment. At the start of 2020, I took early retirement and promised that I would lavish my garden with all the love and attention that it deserved. I had many plans; raised vegetable beds and a greenhouse, alongside filling out tired-looking borders with fresh new plants. Needless to say, the lockdown has meant that my plans are yet to reach fruition. However, my time has been valuably spent reacquainting myself with the bare bones of the garden. I have mulched borders, pruned trees, cleared out dead wood, reinstated the orchard garden with grass borders, restocked and gap-filled the perennial borders, and

> ## "My first reaction was to send my son to our local garden centre with a list."

learned to grow my own veg from seed. I even created a little potager with woven hazel panels from our own coppiced hazel.

WHY WAS YOUR GARDEN SO IMPORTANT DURING LOCKDOWN?

My first reaction when I received notification that I had to shield for 12 weeks was to send my son to our local garden centre with a list of seeds, plants, bulbs and compost. I knew I was going to be locked in all through the key growing season and that my garden needed me and I needed my garden. My overriding lockdown experience was that the garden allowed me to feel safe. I spent endless hours every morning messing about in the soil and then in the afternoon I'd rest in my hammock in the woodland garden, dreaming and making plans for mine and my garden's future.

WHAT IS YOUR BEST MEMORY OF YOUR GARDEN?

Growing my own plants from seed – something I haven't done much of before – and sharing my love of gardening with my two sons, both of whom grew their own lockdown veg along with me via Zoom!

SHARE YOUR FAVOURITE GARDENING ADVICE.

Lift and divide plants. I divided several perennials early in lockdown, potted

them up and I was then able to give them to family and friends as well as create new plant borders for free.

SHARE THE QUIRKIEST THING YOU'VE DONE IN YOUR GARDEN DURING LOCKDOWN?
Star-gazing from my hammock in the woodland garden.

WHAT IS THE ONE THING YOU DISCOVERED DURING LOCKDOWN THAT YOU WILL REPEAT?
I loved growing my own salad crops. I drilled holes in an old tin bath that we used to use to wash our Labrador in and planted a variety of seeds in it. I then made sure that I had a succession of plantings by sowing more seed in lengths of plastic sawn-off guttering pipes. It was the best salad by miles.

WHAT PLANT WOULD YOU NOT BE WITHOUT IN YOUR GARDEN?
I have become totally obsessed with dahlias. At the start of lockdown, I ordered several collections from Sarah Raven's online shop. They are great value for money and flower for weeks and take colour right into autumn. Dahlias also last really well if picked and placed in a vase on the kitchen table. They're the flower that keeps on giving and the range of colours and shapes is out of this world.

YOUR GREATEST GARDENING SUCCESS DURING LOCKDOWN?
My borders have never been so continually full of colour. It was so easy to add colour by shopping for plants online.

"I had COVID-19 very seriously and only just escaped hospital."

Magical movie nights in the garden

We balanced our old projector on books - it wobbled but that added to the fun

@Oldhouseintheshires

Name: Sophie van Gerwen
Location: Wiltshire, England

#weekendgardenparty #gardengreatorsmall #mygardenthismonth

DESCRIBE YOUR GARDEN.

It's a walled country garden that we have created from scratch over the last 5 years. It's rather rambling and relaxed in style but we love that. The theme and planting is cottagey, with a rose garden, small veggie patch, an old apple tree, a wildlife pond and a patio.

Our previous homes have all been typical new builds on estates with tiny gardens, so this property has offered us a very different experience. I've always gardened but this place has enabled me to really get stuck in. We bought the house five years ago as a renovation project, but I've loved creating our garden more than the house.

DO YOU GARDEN ALONE?

My husband and I garden together. Our older teenagers are not very interested!

WHAT WAS YOUR LOCKDOWN LIKE?

We all caught Covid-19, but I had it very seriously and only just escaped hospital. I've been left suffering from 'long Covid', which has been life changing. I've basically been bedbound on and off for four months. My son was in Year 13 in 2020, so he missed his A levels and his driving test. My daughter missed her university exams. It's been tough but we're OK. That's the main thing.

WHY HAS YOUR GARDEN BEEN SO IMPORTANT OVER LOCKDOWN?

It's been a sanctuary and a place to escape the house. With four adults ill at the same time, the garden was a place we could go to get fresh air. For me, it was a place of recovery.

WHAT IS YOUR BEST MEMORY OF YOUR GARDEN?

Having cinema nights outside, using an old projector that we have to balance on books. It works a treat and the fact that it wobbles a bit makes the whole experience more fun. We have also enjoyed eating meals together in the garden, which was wonderful, and once being awake at 4.30am to watch the sun rise.

WHAT'S YOUR FAVOURITE GARDENING ADVICE?

Slugs and snails love dahlias, so I used copper collars (or tops of plastic pots also work well). I also sprinkled wool pellets and nematodes, and I went out at night in search of the pests.

WHAT IS THE ONE THING YOU DISCOVERED DURING LOCKDOWN THAT YOU WILL REPEAT?

Growing my own annuals from seed. I will do this again as it was far easier than I thought. I grew Bells of Ireland (*Moluccella laevis*), cosmos, sweet peas, zinnias, ammi, white lace flower (*Orlaya grandiflora*) and foxgloves.

WHAT IS YOUR TOP RECYCLING TIP?

Pallets. My husband created a new trellis for the pumpkins, a new spinach cage and a new compost bin all from old pallets.

WHAT PLANT CAN'T YOU BE WITHOUT IN YOUR GARDEN?

I can't choose between dahlias and roses. I love dahlias because you go from nothing above ground in March to big, blousy blooms in August. They're so showy and ever so slightly

> **"I've always gardened but this place has enabled me to get stuck in."**

bonkers. Their weird and wonderful names cause entertainment too, especially when they reflect the crazy colour combinations. My favourite that I've grown has to be 'Penhill Watermelon' as each flower was larger than my head! I'm planning on growing more varieties in 2021.

WHAT (OR WHO) HAS BEEN YOUR MOST UNEXPECTED LOCKDOWN GARDEN VISITOR?
We watched two families of blue tits fledge this year. This was so special as usually we miss them due to work. A hedgehog also made a visit to the garden, which was a highlight.

TELL US YOUR GREATEST GARDENING SUCCESS DURING LOCKDOWN.
Growing my dahlias. I'd lifted and stored them from previous years and in lockdown I moved them to a sunny border. This worked really well because I could keep them in pots until they were bigger and stronger before adding them to the garden. Last year we lost 70% of them to slugs and snails so I wasn't taking any chances during lockdown! My husband had to help quite a bit with this due to my ill health.

HAVE YOU GROWN MORE VEGETABLES DURING LOCKDOWN?
We did. We harvested our first strawberries, raspberries, potatoes, spinach, purple beans, rhubarb and later plums, pears and pumpkins. We were inspired due to time, mostly, in all honesty.

"We made an outdoor cinema and snuggled on the garden sofa under blankets."
Roz Vincent @roz_gardens

"I loved sitting in the paddling pool on warm evenings watching the night sky."
Linda Pearce @linda.pearce.7140

"Don't worry too much about getting it right or wrong, just give it a go."
Sue Hopkins @thedorsetbarnacle

Sunny thoughts

"The robin kept coming and sitting with us. So special."
Tina Lovesey @loveseywithlove

"Outdoor space calmed us, added variety and gave us something meaningful to do."
Anna Edwards @greencolourful

"When I was feeling down, just a little potter around the garden lifted my spirits."
Charlotte Tomalin @charlotte.tomalin

"When you are in the garden you become so absorbed, all worries and sense of time disappear."
Jacqui Fox @foxgardening

"I know so much more now about gardening than I did at the start of lockdown."
Sophie Wade @sophiexwade

"The house is smothered with roses to such an extent that you can't actually see out of a sitting room window."

Puppies and petals

A place to relax with my family and dogs and of course, experiment!

@jothompsongarden

❤ 💬 ✈ ⚬ ⚬ ⚬ ⚬ 🔖

Name: Jo Thompson
Location: Sussex, England

DESCRIBE YOUR GARDEN.
When I first moved here, there wasn't a garden, merely a driveway which surrounded the house. Six years later, the new hornbeam hedge now stands at 3.5m and encloses a garden full of colour, with roses and tulips being the stand-out bringers of colour. It isn't always the tidiest – it has to work for a family, for younger children, teenagers and dogs (one old and one puppy). Goalposts sometimes stand on the lawn, and puppies often run into the flower borders at speed. There's a terrace, a new gravel garden and new veg beds and a walkway dripping with roses and clematis. The house is smothered with roses to such an extent that you can't actually see out of a sitting room window. As a landscape architect and garden designer I usually spend more time on other people's gardens and show gardens than my own, but this year was different.

DO YOU GARDEN ALONE?
Dogs are always nearby whilst I'm gardening. Lockdown has increased our teenagers' interest in gardening – miracle!

WHAT WAS YOUR LOCKDOWN EXPERIENCE?
We've been lucky to have had space and to be so near to the countryside. My days were shaped by sharing live #8amdogwalks on Instagram, which Ann-Marie Powell was a great supporter of. We all suddenly had more time to spend in the garden with the sudden lack of a commute. I hadn't spent a May in my garden for 11 years as I'm always away at RHS Chelsea Flower Show creating a garden.

WHAT IS YOUR BEST MEMORY OF YOUR GARDEN?
Sitting outside with that first cup of tea, just as dawn was breaking, listening to the quiet and then listening to the birds joining in the dawn chorus and witnessing their great crescendo of song.

WHAT IS YOUR FAVOURITE GARDENING ADVICE TO SHARE?
A five-pronged slug defence system: raised beds, copper tape, slug fence, wool pellets and beer trap.

TOP UPCYCLE IDEA?
Use Pringle tins to sow sunflower seeds in.

WHAT PLANT WOULD YOU NOT BE WITHOUT IN YOUR GARDEN?
Roses: the scent and colour from April through to October and sometimes longer is so uplifting. I just can't imagine not having roses in my life.

WHAT (OR WHO) HAS BEEN YOUR MOST UNEXPECTED LOCKDOWN GARDEN VISITOR?
A comma butterfly, which visited the same spot near my bench, it seemed, for around three weeks. It would take a perch on my knee, and on Basil the puppy's head. Extraordinary.

YOUR GREATEST GARDENING SUCCESS DURING LOCKDOWN?
My gladioli and sweet peas have been simply glorious this year. Both are great in the garden and wonderful in a vase.

HAVE YOU GROWN MORE VEGETABLES DURING LOCKDOWN?
Salad leaves went down a treat. They grew really well in the four new beds which I quickly put in just as lockdown loomed.

This was the perfect time to tackle the gardening projects we'd talked about for ages

@earthypursuits

Name: Jeanette Gibbs
Location: Worcestershire, England

#artandcraftgardening #gravelgarden
#plantingdesign #lowmaintenanceplants

DESCRIBE YOUR GARDEN.
A large, relaxed country garden, in an elevated position, with open views across rolling Worcestershire countryside. The garden has been subdivided into unique areas by both deciduous and evergreen hedging and traditional paths. These areas include a meadow with a natural pond, a woodland walk, mixed borders and a kitchen garden, with each hopefully reflecting the Arts and Crafts architecture and history of the property.

DO YOU GARDEN ALONE?
This is a family endeavour with my husband, Tim, helping whenever he is home and our son, Joseph, mowing whenever he must. Our daughter, Isla, likes to take on a more observing role.

WHAT WAS YOUR LOCKDOWN EXPERIENCE?
Lockdown was a wake-up call for us. It was really hard hearing the news every day but with so much time on our hands and nowhere to go we decided it was the perfect time to tackle the garden projects we had talked about for years. Without any machinery assistance it was a challenge at times, but we came to enjoy the problem solving, combined effort and the results of our labour. The weather was so kind to us and our connection to nature was really strengthened.

WHY WAS YOUR GARDEN SO IMPORTANT OVER LOCKDOWN?
With what felt like an unrecognisable world around us, our garden became a sanctuary of calm normality, where nature and the seasons ticked along regardless. Simple or hard gardening tasks, they all gave us a purpose and routine, and the satisfaction of achievement each day. We were very aware that many were unable to access the outdoors, so we felt it was important to make good use of what we had, with the whole family spending time together in the garden.

WHAT IS YOUR FAVOURITE GARDENING TIP?
Take lots of photos, to remind yourself of what you have achieved each week/month/year and to help you remember what is planted where when you are planning for next year's scheme over winter.

SHARE THE QUIRKIEST THING YOU'VE DONE IN YOUR GARDEN DURING LOCKDOWN?
Enjoying a Heath Robinson al fresco meal – sitting on a Joseph-made bench, cooking on a Tim-made barbecue, using charcoal they had both made in the garden – and officially naming the barbecue Frank (the old oil tank). "I hereby name…"

WHAT IS THE ONE THING YOU DISCOVERED DURING LOCKDOW THAT YOU WILL REPEAT?
That Instagram could be used for gardening inspiration and support and not just teenage angst!

WHAT IS YOUR TOP RECYCLING TIP?
Pretty much anything can be (and has been) used as a seed tray or pot, including yoghurt pots, toilet rolls, old compost bags, crates etc.

WHAT (OR WHO) HAS BEEN YOUR MOST UNEXPECTED LOCKDOWN GARDEN VISITOR?
A wonderfully noisy cuckoo who decided to perch at the top of our cedar tree to sing out their presence.

"I discovered Instagram was for gardening inspiration and support and not just teenage angst!"

YOUR GREATEST GARDENING SUCCESS DURING LOCKDOWN?
Improved success in propagating (thanks to my 50th birthday present of a greenhouse).

HAVE YOU GROWN MORE VEGETABLES DURING LOCKDOWN?
Yes, lots. The greenhouse and enjoying increased self-sufficiency have inspired us. I particularly enjoyed growing and eating the tricky to find vegetables such as kohl rabi, fennel and Pea 'Blauwschokker'.

Top right: Pea 'Blauwschokker'. The Gibbs family recycled and reused household items wherever they could and kept a photographic record of their ever-changing garden

"A poppy is a pretty profligate plant, and each little pepper pot seed head contains many hundreds of tiny little black dots."

Being a professional gardener means that James often has to focus on other people's gardens but this year his was lavished with love. Right: the spring blooms of magnolias

@JamesASinclair

Name: James Alexander-Sinclair
Location: Oxfordshire, England

2 DAYS AGO

A cascade of colour and buzzing bees

Having a lawn to lie on and borders to tend was an enormous relief

DESCRIBE YOUR GARDEN.

I am a professional gardener: all week I skitter around the place talking to people about gardens. Sometimes I'm asked what I do for relaxation at the weekends and the answer is not skydiving, mud wrestling or naked pottery but ... gardening. This garden is only four years old and will, I hope never, be complete. It has deep borders, a lawn that is annoyingly large (I really do not enjoy cutting grass), a pond that gives great pleasure and a kitchen garden where the chickens live and my wife Celestria grows excellent vegetables. I try never to forget how lucky we are to have such a wonderful garden.

WHY WAS YOUR GARDEN SO IMPORTANT OVER LOCKDOWN?

My garden is always important no matter what is going on or what time of year it may be – but during this particular year knowing that I had a lawn to lie on and a border to get stuck into has been a relief.

YOUR TOP GARDENING TIP?

Never rush – take it slowly. If gardens seem as hectic as real life, then you are doing something wrong!

SHARE THE QUIRKIEST THING YOU'VE DONE IN YOUR GARDEN?

Wearing a kilt whilst talking to Ann-Marie on one of her Instagram lives.

WHAT PLANT WOULD YOU NOT BE WITHOUT IN YOUR GARDEN?

The poppies in my garden are all descended from a single seed head that was given to us by a great friend whose garden had been designed by Dan Pearson (it appeared in a television series called *A Year at Home Farm* – some of you may remember it). A poppy is a pretty profligate plant and each little pepper pot seed head contains many hundreds of tiny little black dots. We took this one home and chucked it around a bit. For the following decade we got more and more flowers, not only in the original dark purple but reds, mauves, pinks and combinations of all of the above. The poppy display became a big part of the year. Then, about five years

ago, we moved house and Celestria brought a few seeds with her. Maybe "a few seeds" is an understatement – she actually brought a sack of seeds which she liberally scattered around the place. As a result, June is a cascade of colour and buzzing bees. Poppies live in the ground for many years so they still will be here giving pleasure long after we have gone.

WHAT (OR WHO) HAS BEEN YOUR MOST UNEXPECTED LOCKDOWN GARDEN VISITOR?

We have had hedgehogs and an unnecessary number of drunk wasps eating windfall pears. Also, a rabbit – while cute in some lights, it is not terribly welcome.

YOUR GREATEST GARDENING SUCCESS DURING LOCKDOWN?

Getting on top of the bindweed – mostly.

HAVE YOU GROWN MORE VEGETABLES DURING LOCKDOWN?

Always beans – easy, useful and delicious. Also, tomatillos: we have a lot of salsa.

Deadhead, deadhead, deadhead! It allows you to enjoy your garden and rewards you with more and more blooms.
Jo Pask @jo.pask

Susie Warwick @susiwar33

Fill bald lawn patches with grass seed sandwiched between wet kitchen paper and cover lightly.

Carolyn Foster @lal.home

Keep an eye out for things that self-seed. They're free and a great way of plants telling us they like their spot!

Hacks, Tips & Tricks

For a blooming marvellous corner of the countryside

Sow more seed than you think you'll need – there's ALWAYS room for more!
Lesley Spicer @sweary.spice

Don't just Chelsea chop – remember to Hampton hack too for a really good second flush of late summer flower.
Angela Arnold @the_hampshire_gardener

@jessicawarman50

Try to keep control of the tomatoes in the greenhouse – nip the tops and side shoots out!

#cottage&country

This bee was spotted in Susan Felton's Northamptonshire garden.

CHAPTER 03

Wildlife, Shade & Woodland

Over lockdown thousands of gardeners took comfort in watching birds, bees, butterflies and bats enjoy their garden. They were welcome guests who could come and go as they pleased.

#wildlifeshade&woodland

Homemade willow and lavender hearts were dropped off anonymously outside local houses to share the joy of the garden.

I've fed the birds and learned bird song

The rejuvenation of the wood has been a major lockdown project

Amanda_gibson_66

Name: Amanda Gibson
Location: Hampshire, England

#gardeningmatters

DESCRIBE YOUR GARDEN.

My garden was once a square 4-acre plot, supposedly the home of the head gardener from the nearby 'big' house way back when. Later, between the wars, the property became a nursery for exotic plants destined for Royal Botanic Gardens, Kew - allegedly! By the time we arrived in 2000, the land had been parcelled out to three new strip-gardened properties, with a wood behind, leaving us with an awkward L-shaped garden. Nature disguised everything with a high tangle of brambles, and almost up to the house were overgrown laurels, firs and self-seeded trees. We set about taming the wilderness and over 20 years have been able to exchange the chainsaw for more conventional garden tools.

The garden has five main areas – raised vegetable beds beside a greenhouse, which is bulging with tomatoes and aubergines in August; a circular lawn bounded by wooden decking with pots, a shrub border and a "hot" sunny bed newly planted during lockdown; a shady area under three lovely *Betula utilis* var. *jaquemontii* (Himalayan birch); a wildlife pond; the chicken/compost corral; and the wood, whose rejuvenation has been a major lockdown activity. Behind the lawn, a gravel path passes from the greenhouse under a pagoda to link the top and bottom gardens.

DO YOU GARDEN ALONE?

I'm the main gardener. My husband isn't into aesthetics; he only grows things he can eat. Our millennial daughters utilise the garden to drink beer or sunbathe.

WHAT WAS YOUR LOCKDOWN EXPERIENCE?

We were thrown out of three countries in a newly acquired motorhome in March! Portugal closed its borders to us, Spain followed and locked-down France calmly hurried us back to Blighty in time for "shall we, shan't we?" UK government lockdown indecision. We were joined by one furloughed daughter and another back from Bristol University. There was nothing for it but to go garden mad. My husband was told "no excuses to not make those pallet compost bins" while I went lumberjacking in the wood and attacked the flower beds.

WHAT IS YOUR BEST MEMORY OF YOUR GARDEN?

I've had the space and time to see plants burst into life; bugs, beetles and bees feeding from flowers; larvae develop into dragonflies. I've fed the birds and learned bird song. I've watched slugs and snails eat my hostas – before Ann-Marie came to the rescue with her garlic spray! I've made my own compost, plant feed and grown plants I've never heard of before.

WHAT IS YOUR FAVOURITE GARDENING TIP YOU'D LIKE TO SHARE?

Liquid comfrey is brilliant plant feed but boy, does it stink! Pack roughly shredded comfrey into a pipe, compress with a water-filled 2 litre plastic bottle attached at the top

#wildlifeshade&woodland

> ## "Our millennial daughters utilise the garden to drink beer or sunbathe."

with string, so it can be pulled out and collect concentrated liquid magic below. We've put a funnel at the bottom.

SHARE THE QUIRKIEST THING YOU'VE DONE IN YOUR GARDEN DURING LOCKDOWN.

Over the Easter weekend I made willow hearts and wrapped them with lavender, then left them anonymously on doors and gates all along our lane and further afield. I hope they made people smile during this hard time. We have lots of bamboo growing in the woodland so I wove a retaining bamboo border in the chicken area. The green bamboo was pliable and did just the job!

WHAT IS THE ONE THING YOU DISCOVERED THAT YOU WILL REPEAT?

Most definitely "Feeding Friday", not that I could ever remember what day

it was in lockdown, such a fab idea to help you regularly remember to feed plants during growing season. Also, deadheading. I can't believe how many plants that have had repeat flowers this year.

WHAT PLANT WOULD YOU NOT BE WITHOUT IN YOUR GARDEN?

Alliums. They produce wonderful colour early in the season and then are fabulous as seed heads in the garden. These seed heads are also useful in flower and foliage arrangements for the house.

WHAT (OR WHO) HAS BEEN YOUR MOST UNEXPECTED LOCKDOWN GARDEN VISITOR?

Wasps! They made a nest in our kettle barbecue on the patio. Unfortunately, because of where it was, we had to get someone in to deal with it, but the nest was an amazing work of art.

YOUR GREATEST GARDENING SUCCESS DURING LOCKDOWN?

My 'Matucana' sweet pea have been incredible this year. I planted the seeds straight from the fridge into cardboard toilet roll tubes filled with my compost. Then I planted them out, only 6, around a homemade tripod made of bamboo. They have flowered for many weeks and I think the colour is amazing.

"Time seemed to disappear when we were in the garden."
Keran Pincombe @a_wold_lifestyle

"Having this much time in my garden was a dream come true."
Teresa Byington @teresabyington

"The introduction of the cut flower border has provided a new focus and has filled the house with blooms."
Ricki Hale @rippy11

Sunny thoughts

"Gardening gave us the exercise and fresh air we needed to keep healthy."
Mary Williams @marywoking

"After about a month of complete isolation a non-gardening friend said on the phone "you must have finished it by now." Gardening is never finished!"
Nichola Henson @Nicholahenson

"Flowers and trees make the garden a little oasis for me to get away from everyone and everything."
Betty-Anne Smith @s.bettyanne

"Lockdown has given me the time and breathing space to learn more about gardening and plants."
Tina Eglington @tinaeglington

"My partner owns a telescope which his maternal grandfather made! During lockdown we enjoyed stargazing together."
Janeen Woodward @janeenwoodward

We spent every waking hour out there

If we stayed in our third floor apartment in Madrid lockdown would've been very different

@angelaridge

❤ 💬 ✈ • • • • •

Name: Angela Ridge
Location: Antwerp, Belgium

2 DAYS AGO

DESCRIBE YOUR GARDEN.

We are located in the suburbs of Antwerp in quite a densely wooded area. Our property is bordered by extremely tall, mature pine trees, oak trees and wild rhododendron. The bones of the garden were here when we bought the property 13 years ago, but it had been neglected. Over time, we have brought it back to life. In the middle of the garden, we have a couple of ponds connected by a small water course which teem with wildlife.

DO YOU GARDEN ALONE?

I like to think that I garden alone. Adrian, my husband, does the hard graft and heavy work. He can also take the credit for the wonderful garden compost that we create.

WHAT WAS YOUR LOCKDOWN EXPERIENCE?

My husband has a very demanding job that takes him all over the world, so we have spent quite a lot of time apart. Lockdown changed that. Our outdoor garden room became Adrian's office, and the garden became mine.

WHAT IS YOUR BEST MEMORY OF YOUR GARDEN?

Our garden during lockdown was our sanctuary. Being immersed in nature is my therapy, having my hands in the soil is pure magic. We could forget what was happening outside our front gates during the time we spent outside, tending to the garden. Fortunately, the weather was more than kind to us and we spent every waking hour out there, having our morning coffee, lunch and dinner and a glass of wine by the pond on our deck some evenings. We felt very grateful to have the garden as our refuge. When we live in Madrid, Spain, we have an apartment on the third floor. If we had stayed there, life would have felt very different.

WHAT IS YOUR FAVOURITE GARDENING ADVICE?

If you're growing *Hydrangea* 'Annabelle', make yourself a "corset" like we did several years ago. It will give the leggy blooms the support that they need.

WHAT (OR WHO) HAS BEEN YOUR MOST UNEXPECTED LOCKDOWN GARDEN VISITOR?

We have four bird boxes in our garden, and we had two clutches of blue tits and two clutches of great tits. We watched the parents feeding them in the nest and then had the honour of seeing them make their first journeys into the garden. We also had a great spotted woodpecker family visit. Sadly, one day one of the babies flew into the window and died instantly. We were heartbroken. My husband buried him under our Japanese lantern where he will rest for eternity.

WHAT IS THE ONE THING YOU DISCOVERED DURING LOCKDOWN THAT YOU WILL REPEAT?

The advice that Ann-Marie gave about weekly feeding fruiting or flowering plants was a real eye opener for me. I had never really fed my plants, other than the roses in spring. Suddenly, I was reaping the rewards.

WHAT PLANT WOULD YOU NOT BE WITHOUT IN YOUR GARDEN?

Hydrangea Annabelle. They came with the house and so have been in our garden for more than 13 years and they just get better and better every year.

> "There is nothing more rewarding than putting back into the earth what came out of it."

Above centre: *Hydrangea* 'Annabelle' with her giant blooms. Other prize plants in the garden are the hostas and the neatly clipped box. The pond is at the heart of the garden and encourages birds to visit the plot.

#wildlifeshade&woodland

There's never a dull moment when you have such a large water feature in the garden. From dawn till dusk wildlife visits and many happy hours have been spent admiring them with the binoculars.

Make a pond and the wildlife will come

The frog chorus on Valentine's Day was one of our most treasured memories

@paulapdavies

Name: Paula Phillips Davies
Location: Carmarthenshire, South Wales
#wildlifegarden #wellbeing #weeds

DESCRIBE YOUR GARDEN.
When we bought the house 22 years ago the garden wasn't much bigger than the footprint of the house itself. This suited us at the time, but in 2013 we bought a plot of land at the rear from the local farmer to give us more outdoor space. It was completely overgrown with brambles, nettles and goat willow (Salix caprea) but we knew that there was a pond in there somewhere. We cleared the site with the intention of creating a wildlife garden. We planted native hedges, mature trees, sowed a wildflower meadow and dug out the pond, to find it was clay-lined and fed by a natural spring. Becoming obsessed with plants, we created a number of zones, taking advantage of the different aspects from sunny, shady, dry and damp. We have a dry garden at the front filled with seashells and plants that can cope with the prevailing winds, then this leads into a more private tropical area filled with tree ferns and palm trees. You then cross a wooden bridge over a small stream through the herb garden to the wildflower meadow, which blends well with the borrowed landscape behind.

DO YOU GARDEN ALONE?
My husband Iain helps me with all the heavy jobs but is happy to potter too.

WHAT WAS YOUR LOCKDOWN EXPERIENCE?
During lockdown, we have been able to enjoy the garden like never before. We have had breakfast in the tropical area, coffee by the pond, lunch in the herb garden, drinks on the top terrace and supper on the balcony – which we've turned into a kitchen garden with our obsession for plants extending to edibles.

WHY WAS YOUR GARDEN BEEN SO IMPORTANT DURING LOCKDOWN?
We had time to admire the visiting wildlife. Our favourite spot of all has to be sitting on the swing chair with binoculars, watching the wildlife in the pond. During lockdown we have observed far more than ever with regular sightings of frogs, newts, damselflies, dragonflies and a lone moorhen. Then, in July, our moorhen brought home a mate and now we have 5 fluffy chicks too.

WHAT IS YOUR BEST MEMORY OF YOUR GARDEN?
There is a saying, make a pond and the wildlife will come. The frog chorus around Valentine's Day is a testament to this and one of our most treasured memories.

DO YOU HAVE A FAVOURITE GARDENING HACK YOU'D LIKE TO SHARE?
Stuff old tights, stockings and pop-socks with barley straw then throw them in the pond to keep the algae down. They do look rather macabre to begin with, floating around like dismembered limbs, but they soon sink!

#wildlifeshade&woodland

"We have had breakfast in the tropical area, coffee by the pond, lunch in the herb garden, drinks on the top terrace and supper on the balcony"

WHAT IS THE ONE THING YOU DISCOVERED DURING LOCKDOWN THAT YOU WILL REPEAT?

That you can make the most of your garden and actually feel like you are on holiday by taking every opportunity to eat and drink outside.

WHAT PLANT WOULD YOU NOT BE WITHOUT IN YOUR GARDEN?

The marsh marigolds *(Caltha palustris)* as they bring such a joyful flash of colour after the long winter months.

WHAT (OR WHO) HAS BEEN YOUR MOST UNEXPECTED LOCKDOWN GARDEN VISITOR?

A huge grass snake – it slithered off into the pond before I could get a photo of it. It was spectacular, truly stunning.

HAVE YOU GROWN MORE VEGETABLES DURING LOCKDOWN?

The edibles growing in pots on the south-facing balcony have been a huge success. We have never done this before but this year we have been self-sufficient in tomatoes, cucumber, salad leaves, chillis, choiggia beetroot, runner beans, parsley, basil and Vietnamese basil.

Visits from the heron and the kingfisher

As a doctor I'm prescribing gardening for mental and physical health

confused at the start of lockdown. Going to work as a doctor every day was scary and isolating. Like many others, I turned to my garden. Using photography – especially close-ups – I started to pay more attention to things, and this helped slow me down and relax after a day at work. I blogged my photos every Saturday morning throughout lockdown. The posts were well received by friends and family. Long story short – I'm now retraining in garden design, but still working in the NHS and loving both.

DESCRIBE YOUR GARDEN.
West facing with heavy clay. I am very lucky to have a big space. When we moved here seven years ago it was all grass, but now we've got lawn, big shady trees, an orchard, paddock, coppicing woodland, veg patch, greenhouse, pond and borders.

DO YOU GARDEN ALONE?
Mrs Claxton and I are a happy team!

WHAT WAS YOUR LOCKDOWN EXPERIENCE?
Like everyone, I was mystified and

WHY WAS YOUR GARDEN SO IMPORTANT OVER LOCKDOWN?
Here goes... outdoor space, Vitamin D, physical exercise, mental health and wellbeing, working with nature, self-sufficiency, biodiversity, food chain, ecology, reducing food transport, reducing pesticides, self-esteem, creativity, beauty, sharing with the wider community (produce, flowers, preserves, photographs, experience). Mainly, whatever awful things were happening in the world, the garden gave us a sense of place, tradition, nature, the cycle of the seasons and an affirmation that life goes on.

WHAT IS YOUR BEST MEMORY OF YOUR GARDEN?
Early morning check-ins with my camera. Peace, tranquillity and a constantly changing range of things happening out there to surprise me. Properly seeing bergenia flowers for the first time. Or evenings; sitting by the pond watching the pipistrelles in the dusk. Seeing a barn owl quartering the paddock. Sunsets and sunrises.

WHAT IS YOUR FAVOURITE GARDENING TIP?
I've got more than one. The first is to recycle old sandwich bags to enclose pots with softwood cuttings. When sealed over a pot my success rate was radically improved. The best advice I've had is gain confidence by realising that there are no failures when gardening – each failure only leads you to learn something new. Lastly, that the sun will rise in the morning.

SHARE THE QUIRKIEST THING YOU'VE DONE IN YOUR GARDEN DURING LOCKDOWN?
Late-night music and dancing on the patio.

WHAT IS THE ONE THING YOU DISCOVERED DURING LOCKDOWN THAT YOU WILL REPEAT?
I intend to stay involved with the

#wildlifeshade&woodland

"Long story short – I'm now retraining in garden design, but still working in the NHS and loving both."

By taking close-up photographs of flowers you get to know and admire the fine details of each bloom. First thing in the morning is the best time to head out with the camera.

Instagram gardening community. It's just lovely to connect with people all around the world, sharing and experiencing their ups and downs together.

WHAT IS YOUR TO RECYCLING IDEA?

Bob Flowerdew's legendary car tyre planters are hard to beat, especially for potatoes. Making a compost heap out of pallets and using squares of old carpet as a porous cover for them.... and, of course, making the compost itself.

WHAT PLANT WOULD YOU NOT BE WITHOUT IN YOUR GARDEN?

Rainbow chard. All year colour and nourishment.

WHAT (OR WHO) HAS BEEN YOUR MOST UNEXPECTED LOCKDOWN GARDEN VISITOR?

The heron and kingfisher have visited (little and large). We suspect they love the newts in our pond.

YOUR GREATEST GARDENING SUCCESS DURING LOCKDOWN?

Maintaining my sanity!

HAVE YOU GROWN MORE VEGETABLES?

Yes. I've grown more to save money, improve my health, for self-esteem and for better taste. Asparagus (so worth the space and the wait....) lettuce, beetroot, cucumbers, onions, peas, beans, garlic, tomatoes, globe artichokes, chard, chillies, rhubarb, herbs, currants, strawberries, raspberries, celeriac, spuds, spuds, spuds.

#wildlifeshade&woodland

Growing hope

What our gardens mean to us

@bpoklecki

Name: Branka Poklecki
Location: Bratina, Zagreb county, Croatia

@vi_and_rose

Name: Sam Hall
Location: Haddenham, Buckinghamshire, England

Our shelter, our country house

In Croatia, lockdown started on 15 March 2020. School was online and pretty much everybody started to work from home. We live in Zagreb, the capital of Croatia and our country house in Bratina is our weekend getaway. Strange as it is, we have always considered our country house a real home, our shelter – not knowing that this year it actually was going to be. On 22 March a strong earthquake hit Zagreb – 5.6 on the Richter scale. After half an hour another strong one hit again. This was the strongest earthquake recorded here in last 140 years. Historical buildings, hospitals and homes in the city centre were ruined. People were in fear of COVID-19 and further quakes, and it was snowing heavily even though it was almost the end of March. Zagreb was shaken more than 100 times. As a result, we decided to move to our country house.

Every day we were planting, gardening, exploring the forest and trying to push away anxiety that was coming through daily news. It was hard to purchase seeds and plants. I reused and planted whatever I could find and spent hours looking for online garden shops that offered delivery. Luckily, we were able to experience some benefits of life in the countryside. Eggs, meat, cottage cheese and cream were purchased from neighbours. Nevertheless, we were missing friends and family. For myself, @myrealgarden was the perfect way to get away from all the bad news and hear people talking about plants with great enthusiasm. It was a certain comfort and I'm amazed how we became a community that was able to share happiness.

Gardening kept me busy. Seeing changes in the garden gave me hope and assured me that time was passing faster to better times. We have been left with happy memories of life in the countryside.

> **"On 22 March a strong earthquake hit Zagreb – 5.6 on the Richter scale."**

A place to cry

Lockdown went from being a strange, unsettling time to one of extreme sadness when my dear dad, who was diagnosed with leukaemia at Christmas, sadly died in June. He had been responding well to chemotherapy treatment but was unable to continue due to Covid-19. We could not be with him as he was shielding on the Isle of Wight; we could only watch on our family Skype calls as he became unwell. He went into hospital for a blood transfusion at the end of May and never came home. We feel extremely lucky that we were able to spend the last four days of his life with him at a wonderful hospice.

With Dad being so ill and then passing away, and having two children to home school, the garden was the place I went to calm down or have a cry. I would be on the phone every day trying to work out what was happening with my father and then having to relay the news to my sisters and brother. I would often march off

Sharp learning curve for a teacher

I teach 5th grade at a public elementary school. During lockdown I was spending a tremendous amount of time in front of screens, being sedentary, stressed, and anxious. I felt like there needed to be a place for me to escape to every once in a while, but I didn't have one. So, I made one! I needed to have this for my sanity, my mental and physical health, and as a way to move away from the computer screen into "real" life! I love learning new things and learning about gardening and plants certainly revived me and my spirit.

My backyard garden was born during the COVID lockdown. For about 5 years the backyard area was all grass from fence to fence. No wildlife, birds, bugs... nothing. My 19-year-old son and I dug up and created a border, put in raised beds, and took apart old dresser drawers to make flower boxes out of. Within these 5 months we've now noticed there's a rabbit, squirrels, chipmunks, many different birds, and finally bees, coming to visit our backyard. This is now a part of our home that we just stare at for hours, marvelling at the bounty the earth has bestowed upon us. I'm very new at all this but, based on the orders I have placed for books, seeds, bulbs, and fertiliser, I know this will be an integral part of my life going forward.

"Gardening and plants revived me and my spirit."

@flower14570

Name: Christine Casagrande
Location: Ludlow, Massachusetts, USA

2 DAYS AGO

"I would often march off down to the bottom of the garden and slowly the anxiety would get easier."

down to the bottom of the garden to weed or sow and slowly the anxiety would get easier. Listening to Ann-Marie's daily chats was a huge help and distraction.

The family enjoyed the space we have here. We loved swinging in the hammock, making home-made pizzas, playing games and sleeping in a friend's tent, listening to the owls.

#wildlifeshade&woodland

A daily routine bought results

@paulawhite7576

Name: Paula White
Location: Cheshire, England

#myrealgarden

DESCRIBE YOUR GARDEN.
I like to call it formal hedgerow. I love classic herbaceous borders, but don't want the restraint that comes with unmoving formality. I prefer the planting to be a bit looser and I like to move things around to keep it fresh and interesting, discovering new plants alongside my favourites and at the same time encouraging wildlife.

DO YOU GARDEN ALONE?
Yes, but I do love helping friends and colleagues to get the best out of their gardens too and help to spark their interest. That excites me.

WHAT WAS YOUR LOCKDOWN EXPERIENCE?
I was very lucky to have been furloughed, not everybody was in that position, nor did everyone have an outside space that they could use as a sanctuary or place to develop to give that much needed project when there was little else to do. So, I have to say that it was a positive for me, in that it gave me time.

WHY HAS YOUR GARDEN BEEN SO IMPORTANT OVER LOCKDOWN?
My garden offered me a different kind of structure from my usual working day. I can only say how it made me feel, really – calm from the daily observation of new growth with tea (or wine!) in hand; the joy of the physical shifting of lawn (my reclamation scheme!) to create a new veg or flower bed and the satisfaction that brought.

WHAT IS YOUR BEST MEMORY OF YOUR GARDEN?
Being able to commit to it daily and seeing the results from that. I feel like I've got to know the garden better and love it more for that.

WHAT IS YOUR FAVOURITE GARDENING HACK?
I have a selection of pots with grasses, gladioli, or pretty much whatever I'm currently growing to drop into 'holes' in the border from remedial work or just plain old trampling! It gives a quick refresh and is good for trying new combinations too.

WHAT IS YOUR TOP RECYCLING TIP?
I use bubble wrap to line my large clay pots before I plant up, and use chunks of polystyrene as crocks in the bottom.

WHAT PLANT WOULD YOU NOT BE WITHOUT?
I thought that would be hard to answer until I looked outside. It has to be eupatorium (the gravel root). It attracts an army of very welcome pollinators and adds height to the border in late summer.

WHAT (OR WHO) HAS BEEN YOUR MOST UNEXPECTED LOCKDOWN GARDEN VISITOR?
I've had coaltits and robins in my nesting boxes for the first time and befriended a scruffy looking blackbird whom I named Bernard.

YOUR GREATEST GARDENING SUCCESS DURING LOCKDOWN?
The newest flower border took me by surprise. I'm usually a foliage, texture and green girl, but I fell in love with colour again.

HAVE YOU GROWN MORE VEGETABLES DURING LOCKDOWN?
I hadn't grown veg for about 20 years, because I work away so much, so it was fantastic to pick French beans, salad leaves, herbs and courgettes this year.

> "I feel like I've got to know the garden better and love it more for that."

Creating a new flower bed allows you to play with plant combinations and have fun buying and growing new plants. It's a way of putting your own stamp on the garden.

#wildlifeshade&woodland

Hacks, Tips & Tricks

For a wonderfully wildlife-friendly retreat

Cultivate a sanctuary by living in harmony with wildlife. We love sharing our garden with our resident hare and her family.
Ellie Luk @gascon_gardener

@anthepan

Anna Cox
Go with the wild and unkempt. Our meadow is entirely self-sown apart from our introduction of yellow rattle.

A small hedgehog that came to drink at our pond also eats snails off the lettuce!
Martina Vollbrecht @Martina.Vollbrecht

Single flowers in sunny colours attract pollinators. Wildlife friendly and looks good too!
Jackie Peck @jackiepeck7

Enjoy family time spent in the garden, playing, celebrations, afternoon tea, eating outside and watching wildlife together.
Rachel McLeod @rachelm9229

I garden organically in Canada so everywhere teems with birds and insects (but also skunks and raccoons, which I wish I could discourage!)
Ann Brodie @troisfleches3

@doolintracey

Tracey Doolin
Mix wildflower seeds with sand, rake them into the soil and the resulting flowers will attract lots of pollinating insects and give you flowers to pick.

Teacher Charlotte Sampson used the garden to entertain, teach and excite her children.

CHAPTER 04

Grow Your Own

Why head to the shops when you can pop outside and pick your own lunch?
Where there is room for a pot there is the opportunity to grow edibles.
Theses gardeners feasted as a result of their efforts.

#growyourown

We've experimented and learnt through trial and error

@monty_titchmarsh_hamilton ...

Name: Sam and Tom Leavesley-Matthews
Location: Bewdley, England

#savethebutterflies #growyourown

DESCRIBE YOUR GARDEN.

Tom: We have a small dormer-bungalow with about 6m x 10m of back garden that we share with two dogs – and soon will share with our son, too. The garden was a deck and a muddy slope when we arrived here in 2018. We wanted a space that would work for everyone. As a result, we have created spaces for us to work in, rest, play and grow as much as we can possibly fit in using terraces, pots and raised beds. This is our first proper garden as we rented before and only had about a metre square of terrace, so although this garden is small it offers plenty more opportunities than we are used to.

DO YOU GARDEN ALONE?

Sam: We spend time individually and together as often as we can in our garden. I have been lucky enough to enjoy being in the garden and gardening for as long as I can remember. My grandad was a sculptor and keen gardener. I spent hours looking for stag beetles and frogs amongst the ivy and statues. Growing up, I had a wonderful neighbour who I loved to hang over the fence and chat to about her garden. Tom started vegetable gardening very recently when I bought him some raised beds for his birthday. Since then we have enjoyed gardening together.

WHAT WAS YOUR LOCKDOWN EXPERIENCE?

Sam: We have both continued to work but have had very little of the extra pressures work brings. I am a primary school teacher and Tom is Partnerships Manager for a charity. This extra time has allowed us to be creative, to find some head space, routine and enjoyment of watching the seasons change in the garden.

WHY WAS YOUR GARDEN SO IMPORTANT OVER LOCKDOWN?

Tom: The contact with nature, the changing seasons, growing food and having room to breathe has been invaluable during this time. We feel very lucky to have the space we have.

WHAT IS YOUR BEST MEMORY OF YOUR GARDEN?

Sam: For me, it has been making kimchi from my own Chinese cabbages.
Tom: My best memory has been growing and harvesting a bumper crop of chillies.

WHAT GARDENING ADVICE WOULD YOU LIKE TO SHARE?

Sam: Keep a record of what has worked and what hasn't, enjoy the successes and don't let the setbacks get you down. There's always something that will grow well in your garden – it's just a case of finding it and experimenting.

SHARE THE QUIRKIEST THING YOU'VE DONE IN YOUR GARDEN DURING LOCKDOWN?

Tom: We set ourselves up to watch the Starlink satellites in the middle of the night. We spent ages waiting for them... and finally realised it was the wrong night!

WHAT IS THE ONE THING YOU DISCOVERED DURING LOCKDOWN THAT YOU WILL REPEAT?

Sam: Zinnias are stunning annuals that are easy to grow from seed. They keep flowering right into late summer.
Tom: Grow veg that will make a

Pots and raised beds are planted with a mix of edibles and ornamentals happily rubbing shoulders. A visit from a hummingbird hawk-moth adds to the excitement (below).

#growyourown

> "We have a plant-based diet and anything we can grow ourselves is a treat."

difference to you. Cavolo Nero cabbage is expensive to buy but so easy to grow in large robust quantities. Sow from seed anytime from April through to June – this loose-leaf cabbage is great in a stir fry.

WHAT IS YOUR TOP UPCYCLE OR RECYCLING IDEA?

Sam: Rainwater harvesting is essential for container gardeners as it making your own compost.

WHAT PLANT WOULD YOU NOT BE WITHOUT IN YOUR GARDEN?

Sam: *Verbena bonariensis* – these stunning plants with purple flowers and wiry stems grow well in our soil and knit our whole garden together. They attract a huge variety of pollinators and self-seed easily.

WHAT (OR WHO) HAS BEEN YOUR MOST UNEXPECTED LOCKDOWN GARDEN VISITOR?

Sam: The hummingbird hawk-moth! In 36 years neither of us had ever seen one. They prefer to fly in the daylight and their wings beat so fast that they create a hum. Apparently, it's scented plants such as honeysuckle and buddleja that attract them to the garden in summer.

YOUR GREATEST GARDENING SUCCESS DURING LOCKDOWN?

Tom: This year the vegetable garden has really taken off. We have a plant-based diet and anything we can grow ourselves is a treat. It's the challenge and curiosity of growing veg that we both enjoy. The garden is small so we have tried to grow a limited but high-cropping range of foods. Staples have been Cavolo Nero, chard, beetroot, broad beans and tomatoes.

Sam: Our favourite recipe from the garden this year has been vegan kimchi with homegrown Daikon radish (a large white radish) and Chinese cabbage. The cabbage is salted heavily for a couple of hours, then the moisture is squeezed out. Then mix a porridge of onion, garlic, sugar and Korean pepper flakes then thickened with rice flour. Mix in with ginger, carrot and radish matchsticks. Coat the cabbage and put in a jar to ferment. Burp the jar until it has calmed down. Lasts in the fridge if you can resist eating it all.

Growing hope

What my garden means to me

@Liz.meyer109

Name: Liz Meyer
Location: North East Lincolnshire, England

success – to fill the gaps. I realised that the garden and gardening was essential to my happiness and mental well-being and that I shouldn't be afraid to spend money on it and ask for help when I needed it. I also enjoyed the camaraderie of new online friends and local plant swappers.

A highlight for us was doing physiotherapy sessions in the garden with our little girl. We had been told she would never walk or stand unaided.

> "A highlight for us was doing physiotherapy sessions in the garden, with our little girl."

A place of hope

I have been shielding a little girl with palliative care needs, whom we have made a lifetime fostering commitment to. Consequently, the @myrealgarden community has been my source of joy through some really dark times. Before lockdown much of the garden was neglected, as I've been unwell with a chronic health condition for years. Then, as we couldn't go out much and my husband was working from home, we turned to the garden for entertainment and exercise. We repaired the vegetable patch, pulled out weeds, sowed old seeds that had been lurking in the drawers, swapped plants with neighbours and ordered online – with varying degrees of

#growyourown

Drama down the allotment

Everything was ready to go but my plans were unexpectedly crushed

Name: Beverley Setchell
Location: Norfolk, England

#myrealgarden #allotment

DESCRIBE YOUR GARDEN.

A 1953 detached house on a plot of nearly half an acre. The front garden faces the road and is just lawn, shrubs and trees. I am planning to create a meadow on the front lawn next year. The rear garden is currently three large perennial herbaceous borders, two of which are surrounded by low box hedging. Apple trees, new lockdown mini allotment area, greenhouse, fruit cage, fernery, ornamental cherry trees, Indian bean trees (catalpas) and lots of mint. My three-year-old granddaughter and I always seems to be chewing on a mint leaf!

WHAT WAS YOUR LOCKDOWN EXPERIENCE?

In November I secured a brilliant allotment and had prepared it ready for spring planting. I roped my husband in to add height to the existing fences as muntjac deer are a problem on the allotment and in our garden. It was all set to go – I had seeds, plants, chitting potatoes, onion sets ready to go – when the previous tenant reappeared disputing the tenancy. They stripped it of everything; all the fencing, two greenhouses, a shed, the paving and water butt. It really knocked me for six – you'd have thought there'd been a death in the family, tears and everything.

Lockdown gave us time to clear the bottom of our garden and get planting everything I had ready for the plot. The result was way too many potatoes! Despite the drama and delay, I do now have the allotment plot as a blank canvas for next year.

WHAT IS YOUR BEST MEMORY OF YOUR GARDEN?

We put up a square hazel structure and planted it with sweet peas, *Cobaea scandens*, morning glory (ipomoea) and climbing nasturtiums. It's right outside my greenhouse and a great place to sit for a tea break whilst watching the bees do their thing.

WHAT IS YOUR FAVOURITE GARDENING HACK?

Use an upturned pallet for storing bamboo canes.

SHARE THE QUIRKIEST THING YOU'VE DONE IN YOUR GARDEN DURING LOCKDOWN?

My husband fashioned a Norwegian log candle for a nice evening of sitting out with a glass or two. Then it set fire to the dried lawn, so that was short-lived!

WHAT DID YOU DISCOVER DURING LOCKDOWN THAT YOU WILL REPEAT?

Connection with the soil, self-sufficiency and keeping in touch with the amazing gardening community I've discovered during lockdown.

WHAT PLANT WOULD YOU NOT BE WITHOUT IN YOUR GARDEN?

I love a cosmos – all shapes/colours. They just keep giving; they're easy to grow from seed and flower right up until autumn arrives.

YOUR GREATEST GARDENING SUCCESS DURING LOCKDOWN?

Introducing more colour by adding a cutting garden alongside the veg garden. The dahlias looked amazing here.

HAVE YOU GROWN MORE VEGETABLES DURING LOCKDOWN?

Yes. I'm really pleased with my first planting of kohl rabi. Love it – amazing colour, shape and flavour. Will be repeating next year.

"You'd have thought there'd been a death in the family, tears and everything."

(left) A hazel structure was put up over which annual climbers such as sweet peas, morning glory and climbing nasturtiums climbed. The result was a tunnel of flowers.

#growyourown

Even with limited DIY skills you can recycle and produce eclectic items that are useful in the garden. More rewarding than chucking things in a skip and makes your garden more individual.
Kerry Connolly @willowandgreene2019

Amazing Upcycling

When shopping wasn't possible gardeners got creative and made use of vintage and recycled items

Pallets are amazing to use to make containers for plants and compost bins.
Mary Williams @marywoking

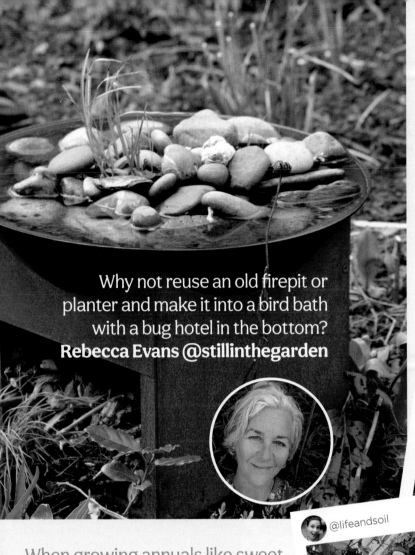

Why not reuse an old firepit or planter and make it into a bird bath with a bug hotel in the bottom?
Rebecca Evans @stillinthegarden

You can plant anything that holds soil! I try to find a way to recycle everything, from my son's wheelbarrow to the bathroom sink.
Piper Hocking @piper_hocking

When growing annuals like sweet peas, reuse your written labels by soaking them in water with a drop of bleach – it even fetches off permanent marker.
Jack D'Arcy @agardenerspassionpot

@lifeandsoil

Lisa Camlin
Upcycle pallets! We have used pallets in the garden to make garden gates, stools and even a garden sofa. This is the perfect spot to sit at the end of a hard day's work in the garden. Our next project is to try to make some loungers.

We lived outside for the whole weekend

The children planned our meals around what we had grown in the garden

@all.home.grown

❤ 💬 ✈   🔖

Name: Charlotte Sampson
Location: Hampshire, England

#flowersfrommygarden
#mygardenthismonth

DESCRIBE YOUR GARDEN.

The garden is a happy jumbled mess of colour, scent, food and flowers, with places to hide, eat, drink and socialise. My husband is fantastic at creating my vision; I would say our garden design is rustic and his building techniques reflect this. We have added split chestnut fencing, arches and pergola; chestnut raised beds; he has built a shepherds hut, a mismatched patio from old stones and bricks and this year he built me a greenhouse shed from reclaimed and recycled wood and a veg garden with raised beds. We are very lucky that our farm, and so house and garden are on a country estate and so we are completely surrounded by the countryside.

DO YOU GARDEN ALONE?

My grandma and mum are gardeners and I have always had a go at gardening, normally with them helping, but lockdown meant it was just me, my husband and the children.

WHAT WAS YOUR LOCKDOWN EXPERIENCE?

I am a full-time teacher who lets the work-life balance tip in the wrong direction. Lockdown gave me time in the garden after spending the day working from home or in school teaching keyworker's children.

WHY WAS YOUR GARDEN SO IMPORTANT OVER LOCKDOWN?

It's been my place to wind down, to have something to focus on and share with my family. I spent a lot of my time with my own children planting seeds and tending to our vegetable garden. They really enjoyed planning menus around the food we were picking for dinner and then cooking too – the whole process from seed to plate! The key has been letting them choose what we grow. We have grown beans, broccoli, pumpkins, tomatoes, cabbage, sprouts, courgettes, carrots, parsnips and peas.

WHAT IS YOUR BEST MEMORY OF YOUR OWN GARDEN?

Watching things grow from seed with the children – Poppy loved nurturing her poppy seeds, Rosa grew carrots to share with family. At school, I have always run a gardening club. I work with children with special needs and being able to take them into the garden has been brilliant! They helped shift several tons of gravel, weed, build the beds and now planting. They have loved every step and it's created great memories for us all.

SHARE THE QUIRKIEST THING YOU'VE DONE IN YOUR GARDEN DURING LOCKDOWN?

Living outside for the weekend – all food made outside, sleeping in the shepherd's hut, and not allowed to enter the house!

YOUR GREATEST GARDENING SUCCESS DURING LOCKDOWN?

Creating a pond and getting the children hooked on gardening. This year on their Christmas list are new tools and gloves for the garden. Every weekend they ask what job we are going to do. They are hoping to grow our Christmas dinner– sprouts, potatoes, kale, leeks and carrots!

"My girls loved watching their seeds grow and kept diaries for school projects – the garden became a fun place to learn."

By involving the whole family in the planning of the garden it has become a happy space for fun, an outdoor classroom and a place to unwind.

#growyourown

"The garden would be my green therapy and the place for daily exercise."

Cooking as well as gardening kept me entertained. New challenges such as decorating focacci (left) with edibles were great motivators.

Gardeners are never alone

I picked what I needed every day from my garden

@Barbarasegall

Name: Barbara Segall
Location: Suffolk, England

#gardeninglife, #herbsforever,
#growyourown, #smallgarden

DESCRIBE YOUR GARDEN.
My garden is in a town, walled on two sides, with a wooden fence and the house making the third and fourth boundaries. It is small and so everything has to be productive or ornamental or both. I grow herbs, fruit, veg, roses, perennials, and small trees. It is packed with plants and I also grow quite a lot in containers.

DO YOU GARDEN ALONE?
I garden on my own, with occasional help if the task is too heavy.

WHAT WAS YOUR LOCKDOWN EXPERIENCE?
I decided that I had to grow more salads and beans. I knew that I would have to use all the seeds I already had, as supply of new seed would be limited. I used large containers as well as two raised beds solely for veg. I realized I couldn't be totally self-sufficient, but I felt that the garden would be my green therapy and the place for daily exercise. I have a little room outside that I call my "dreaming, thinking, drinking room" and that became the place I started my day with a cup of coffee. It is like a secret hideaway in the garden where I can watch and listen to the birds. I made cordials from lilac, ate and froze fruit, enjoyed fresh beans and salads daily as the summer went on… and while I resisted making sourdough until very late in lockdown, I did make several attempts at focaccia art using herbs and flowers to decorate my dough.

WHY HAS YOUR GARDEN BEEN SO IMPORTANT OVER LOCKDOWN?
I feel so fortunate that I have this outdoor space. I went out each day, got my lungs full of fresh air and had a good garden workout. It was wonderful to have the time to see things grow on a daily basis. I'm a garden writer, so I'm usually rushing around interviewing other gardeners and my own garden in the past came a poor second. Now it is the focus of my daily life. I enjoyed bringing the outdoors in by filling vases with seasonal flowers.

WHAT IS YOUR BEST MEMORY OF YOUR GARDEN?
The first thing I did to make the salad garden plan come to life was to dig out a whole raised bed of wonderful agapanthus. It was back-breaking work over two days, but I did it on my own. Then I filled the bed with new compost and sowed seed and planted plug plants and a few months later started harvesting delicious leaves, beans and tomatoes. And there is more to come…

WHAT IS YOUR FAVOURITE GARDENING TIP YOU'D LIKE TO SHARE?
Sow little and often to keep a good continuity of fresh herbs and salad leaves. I am looking forward to sowing mustard leaves and pak choi, as well as lambs lettuce and spinach to keep me going into the winter. Harvest a little each day, just what you need. And if you have too much of anything offer it to friends and neighbours.

SHARE THE QUIRKIEST THING YOU'VE DONE IN YOUR GARDEN DURING LOCKDOWN?
I joined garden designer Jo Thompson early one morning on International Dawn Chorus day to listen to the birds. It was fun sitting in the garden wrapped in a fleece at an unearthly hour.

#growyourown

"If you live alone and you garden you are never really on your own."

WHAT IS THE ONE THING YOU DISCOVERED DURING LOCKDOWN THAT YOU WILL REPEAT?

That being in the garden and keeping in touch with garden friends brings a great sense of belonging and community. In times like these, if you live alone and you garden, you are never really on your own as there is a ready-made group of people who share your passion for plants and gardening. I will definitely keep in touch with the groups who have been so supportive.

WHAT IS YOUR TOP RECYCLING IDEA?

Re-using old compost at the base of pot when you replant, as well as adding polystyrene (which can't be recycled) to bulk out a pot.

WHAT PLANT WOULD YOU NOT BE WITHOUT IN YOUR GARDEN?

Basil: I grow so many different sorts and one that is perennial, which I overwinter in my small greenhouse.

SHARE YOUR GREATEST GARDENING SUCCESS DURING LOCKDOWN.

Constant fruit and salad harvests, some from new plants and others from an established thornless blackberry. Having this supply of goodies made me more experimental with my cooking.

HAVE YOU GROWN MORE VEGETABLES DURING LOCKDOWN?

I now grow more salads, beans, tomatoes (outdoors), chard, spinach, coriander and parsley. I like eating these veg and herbs fresh. I wanted to grow something productive and useful that would keep my spirits up and my taste buds happy. There is nothing like the taste of fresh, home-grown, in season fruit veg and herbs that you have grown yourself.

Growing hope

What my garden means to me

@laurabonalumiency

Name: Laura Bonalumi
Location: London, England

We kept the plot

Plot 351B was offered to us a few days before the birth of my now 12-year-old daughter, Sofia. It is part of a vast piece of land owned by the beautiful Dulwich College in south-east London. The plot is a few miles away from home, so we cycle there as a family now that the girls are able to ride safely. It is a plastic-free plot, so we try to use bricks, wooden sticks, terracotta pots and chipping on its paths. Everything is grown organically and we do lots of spring digging, add horse manure and sow seeds we have collected ourselves from previous plantings. Our tools are old fashioned – shovels and rakes were bought second hand.

Last March we were about to return the plot as my husband and I were suffering from physical injuries and felt stressed by family commitments and the news around Covid-19. We thought it was the end of our experience. Then one night I randomly watched *Gardeners' World* and it featured Arthur Parkinson showing his front garden. I found Arthur on Instagram and discovered he was speaking on a lunch break to Ann-Marie Powell – and I was absolutely captivated by her. I started following her and day by day I gained confidence in how and what to plant and quickly realised that real gardens aren't like the ones you see on the covers of magazines. As a result, we kept the plot and it became the major highlight of our week. It allowed us to leave the house, ride our bikes and be free in a safe place. At the allotment I was able to calm down, find some peace of mind and recharge for another day of home schooling, working from home and housekeeping.

> **"I quickly realised that real gardens aren't like the ones you see on the covers of magazines."**

"We hung an old sheet up and used a projector to have movie nights outside, however it involved staying up very late until it was dark enough!"

Projector nights allowed us some escape

Over 16 years we have changed the garden to suit our family needs

@eliza.gray.gardens

Name: Eliza Gray
Location: Somerset, England

#growyourown #gardendesign

DESCRIBE YOUR GARDEN.
Our garden is about 10m x 100m, sloping gently away from the house with views across a Somerset valley. The house used to be a cider pub, and the long, sloping garden consisted of just grass, fruit trees and a conifer. Over the 16 years we have been here, we have changed the garden to suit us, and it has evolved into a series of spaces with different styles and functions.

DO YOU GARDEN ALONE?
My husband and I garden, and we bribe the kids to mow the lawn.

WHAT WAS YOUR LOCKDOWN EXPERIENCE?
The first few weeks gave me the opportunity to finally clear a border and plant up my 'lockdown bed', which I had been planning for a year!

We continued to grow veg as we normally do, although being at home has meant that the veg has benefitted from daily attention and we are now enjoying a magnificent bounty.

WHY WAS YOUR GARDEN SO IMPORTANT OVER LOCKDOWN?
The garden provided a space to escape, a focus and sense of purpose for us. When the time was right, it was also a beautiful safe space for us to see friends and family. Being at home meant that we were able to take our lunch in the garden and enjoy morning coffee quietly sitting with the dogs in the sunshine. Rather than using home as a launchpad for our next activity, we have all felt connected and grounded spending more time in the garden. Our youngest son built a pond, and our eldest son had a socially distanced camp out as restrictions relaxed. As the seasons changed, it has helped us to feel that some parts of life were going on as normal.

WHAT IS YOUR BEST MEMORY OF YOUR OWN GARDEN?
The early morning wander down the garden in the spring this year will always be etched into my memory. The peace during lockdown meant that a coffee first thing in

the morning in the garden with the dogs was a very special time. The phenomenal weather, heightened sense of the moment and experience of nature unfolding will be crystal clear in my memory for many years to come.

WHAT IS YOUR FAVOURITE GARDENING TIP?
Underplant your broad beans with kale – it keeps the pests off until the kale is robust enough to cope alone. And add chicken poo in February!

SHARE THE QUIRKIEST THING YOU'VE DONE IN YOUR GARDEN DURING LOCKDOWN?
For my birthday I was given a projector. We rigged up a sheet for film night, but could not start the film until it was dark at 10pm – we ended up having to go to bed midway through the film as we are all lightweights!

WHAT IS THE ONE THING YOU DISCOVERED DURING LOCKDOWN THAT YOU WILL REPEAT?
Feeding Friday really does make a huge difference.

WHAT IS YOUR TOP RECYCLING IDEA?
With garden centres closed for the crucial period across March and April, I have absolutely loved living in our local community. We have all swapped seeds, cuttings, pots and

> "The early morning wander down the garden in the spring this year will always be etched into my memory."

plants and really enjoyed sharing. Although this is not strictly recycling, I truly felt that we were embracing the spirit of 'waste not want not' and making the most of what we had.

WHAT PLANT WOULD YOU NOT BE WITHOUT IN YOUR GARDEN?
I expect that most people have chosen a beautiful flower, such as an astrantia but I have to be honest and say rhubarb. 'Timperley Early' was in fruit just when we all needed a boost in March. rhubarb gin anyone?

TELL US YOUR MOST UNEXPECTED LOCKDOWN GARDEN VISITOR.
Soon after the pond was created, my son was delighted and slightly terrified to spot a snake sunbathing!

YOUR GREATEST GARDENING SUCCESS DURING LOCKDOWN?
The 'Lockdown Border' has totally exceeded my expectations. I am extremely pleased that I have finally planted up the group of *Hydrangea* 'Annabelle' that have been waiting in a side bed for nearly a year.

HAVE YOU GROWN MORE VEGETABLES DURING LOCKDOWN?
We have always grown veg here, but we did dig extra beds for more potatoes this year and were much better at watering and succession sowing as we were at home more. The broad beans were fantastic and very tasty the early warm weather has meant that the cucumbers are profligate too.

@bridgetlgalloway

Name: Bridget Galloway
Location: Oxford, England

2 DAYS AGO

Badgers ate most of our carrots

Our allotment gave us plenty to feast on and be proud of

DESCRIBE YOUR GARDEN.

I have a small west-facing garden at the back of our terraced house and an allotment five minutes walk away on the banks of the River Thames. The back garden gets some afternoon sun, but shade tolerant plants do best due to all the surrounding buildings. It has acers, hydrangeas, ferns and a climbing rose. Lots of clematis help blur the boundaries. Heucheras provide year-round interest and the gaps are filled with perennials and bulbs especially tulips, alliums and lilies.

We have had our allotment for 20 years. It floods most years, although we always live in hope and try some winter crops. However, the flooding gives us the excuse to leave some of the plot as grass, giving it a garden feel and I also grow lots of flowers on the allotment. I love being able to pick flowers in abundance for our house and to give away. We grow a wide variety of vegetables. We have a greenhouse crammed full of seedlings in the spring, which we later fill with tomatoes

– probably my favourite edible crop. Black Krim (Tomato 'Noire de Crimée') are the tastiest, but we try different ones every year. We are less successful when it comes to soft fruit but do have several fruit trees.

DO YOU GARDEN ALONE?

The allotment is a joint activity with my husband, Simon, but the back garden is my own work (apart from the lawn mowing!)

WHAT WAS YOUR LOCKDOWN EXPERIENCE?

I'm a doctor, so I continued to go to work. It was a challenging time with lots of decision making for GPs, as we changed virtually overnight to a telephone-first service and ensured that our staff could work remotely where possible. Our two

teenage sons also needed support with homeschooling. Luckily, we have had access to beautiful outdoor spaces and one silver lining was the opportunity to exercise with our boys when they were unable to see their friends. I was so relieved that the allotments were not closed. I had already ordered seeds and was able to use local shops for mail-order compost and plants.

WHY WAS GARDENING SO IMPORTANT OVER LOCKDOWN?

Daily visits to the allotment were a lifesaver. I have always found gardening to be absorbing and relaxing. Our back garden, as small as it is, provided additional space for us all to use when we were unable to go out much. It's been used for sitting in and reading, eating or practising gymnastics (hence the bald patch in the lawn).

WHAT IS YOUR BEST MEMORY OF YOUR GARDEN OR ALLOTMENT?

A June evening barbecue on the allotment after a swim in the Thames, eating our own fresh veg, sitting surrounded by beautiful flowers. I felt very blessed watching the sun set.

#growyourown

WHAT IS YOUR FAVOURITE GARDENING ADVICE?

Make the most of self-seeded plants (they're free) but be brave enough to thin them out so that the plants have enough space to thrive.

SHARE THE QUIRKIEST THING YOU'VE DONE IN YOUR GARDEN DURING LOCKDOWN?

When the gyms closed, our son Will came to the allotment and created his own weights out of two garden trugs filled with water and an old steel bar. And both he and his brother showed that you are never too old for an Easter egg hunt in the back garden.

WHAT IS THE ONE THING YOU DISCOVERED DURING LOCKDOWN THAT YOU WILL REPEAT?

We invested in proper protection for our brassicas. Even if it resulted in

the most expensive broccoli and kale we have ever eaten, it was worth doing.

WHAT PLANT WOULD YOU NOT BE WITHOUT IN YOUR GARDEN?

So difficult to pin it down to one, but it would be hydrangeas in the back garden and sunflowers on the allotment. We grew sunflowers in our first year there for our September wedding and have continued to do so ever since.

WHAT (OR WHO) HAS BEEN YOUR MOST UNEXPECTED LOCKDOWN GARDEN VISITOR?

Badgers, who ate most of our precious carrots. I hope they enjoyed then!

"Daily visits to the allotment have been a lifesaver."

HAVE YOU GROWN MORE VEGETABLES DURING LOCKDOWN?

We have always grown lots on our allotment but this year more than ever. Our glut of courgettes fed the neighbourhood. Other successes: autumn-sown broad beans, drought-tolerant Swiss chard 'Lucullus', flower sprouts and tomatoes. Not so successful: peas (but can't stop trying) and carrots (badgers got there first).

Our garden is very small so having an allotment allowed us to grow cut flowers and crops. The garden was used for exercise - hence the bare patch on the lawn (right).

@the_little_plot_of_dreams

Make watering easy. I'm thrilled with my well-scrubbed oil-drum water-gathering system.
Krissie Sorel-Cameron
@krissiesorelcameron

Hazel Southam
Grow what you like eating. It's remarkable how many people don't. Whatever you love to eat, try growing it, and apply that to all seasons.

Hacks, Tips & Tricks

For a happy home-grown harvest

Nature is good for the soul! Enjoy growing your plants but also storing them as pickles and chutneys in jars for your cellar.
Eveline Aregger
@arreggereveline

Share any fruit and veg surplus with friends and neighbours. It's a cliché, but it really is so rewarding.
Christine Smith @plot.66

Grow Tromboncino, you won't regret it! Tastes great when eaten small and stores well once large (like a squash), and it looks beautiful too.
@londongardenadvice Maximo Cabeza

Grow flowers with your vegetables, which will look pretty and also attract the pollinators.
Pauline Chapman @paulinechapmanleek

@peacocksmith

RHUBARB

Becca Smith
Expand your culinary repertoire. Food you've grown in your garden is so yummy – we especially enjoyed the homemade rhubarb gin and the rhubarb and ginger jam.

Jain Keenan-Livingstone's new Victorian style front path offers a dramatic welcome

CHAPTER 5

Front Gardens

The often ignored front garden has suddenly become a place that allows gardeners to share their passion and stay in touch with the community.

We transformed the garden from just gravel into something very special

@birdhouse_and_bench

Name: Jain Keenan-Livingstone
Location: Belfast, Northern Ireland

#myrealgarden
#mygardenthismonth

DESCRIBE YOUR GARDEN.

I have a north-facing front garden and small south-facing back garden attached to a semi-detached Victorian property in a city. The catalyst for beginning a new project was the removal of a tall hedge at the front of the house. It was such a huge task to keep it clipped so the plan was to replace it with a Victorian style chequered path and wrought iron railings. Installation of the railings and tiling of the path were effected when the lockdown restrictions were put in place and work had to stop, as materials to complete the hard landscaping became unavailable. As a result, my initial plan to create a new spring garden over the weeks during lockdown quickly changed to a late summer/autumn garden. When I say plans, what I really mean is that the planting was dictated by what was available at the garden centre at the time.

DO YOU GARDEN ALONE?

I garden with my husband, Ian. We grew up together, raised a family together and continue to grow our garden together, even if he has pruned and weeded things he should have left well alone. In 2018 Ian was diagnosed with abdominal cancer and my priorities were elsewhere, so the garden became overgrown and overwhelming. This time to focus on the garden was just what we needed. 2020 saw us celebrating our 30th wedding anniversary.

WHAT WAS YOUR LOCKDOWN EXPERIENCE?

The most positive aspect of lockdown for me was being given 'permission' to slow down and recuperate from the stresses of the previous year that had been marked by illness and uncertainty in the family. Before lockdown I was working full time, providing support to families in need, and also helping my sister, who is a nurse and true NHS hero, in caring for our mum who has complex health needs as well as dementia. I'm sure I was heading for a breakdown. Lockdown gave me time and glorious weather to focus solely on getting the garden back into shape.

WHY HAS YOUR GARDEN BEEN SO IMPORTANT OVER LOCKDOWN?

Many will identify with the quote attributed to Audrey Hepburn that, "To plant a garden is to believe in tomorrow"; I'm definitely an optimistic person and my garden helped me to remain positive. For me lockdown highlighted the importance of cherishing your friends and family, taking the rough with the smooth, and hopefully coming through the uncertainty. Gardening gave me such joy and satisfaction.

WHAT IS YOUR BEST MEMORY OF YOUR GARDEN?

Spring and early summer were glorious, with unbroken sunshine and so much time to enjoy it. I was out there from early morning until evening. Discovering @myrealgarden was a game changer. Lockdown routines and activities were arranged around the

The removal of a large hedge has let more light into the north-facing front garden giving opportunities to grow a larger variety of plants in this now much brighter space.

#frontgardens

'Lunchtime Lives'. Meeting so many gardeners from far and wide has been exciting.

WHAT IS YOUR FAVOURITE GARDENING ADVICE YOU'D LIKE TO SHARE?

Although I love the garden to look pretty, my plants need to be tough and able to survive with minimal intervention from me. I've made a lot of mistakes over the years, putting the wrong plants in the wrong places, and learned the hard way that life is a lot simpler having plants that thrive in the existing conditions. This is particularly challenging in a shady, north-facing garden.

TELL US THE QUIRKIEST THING YOU'VE DONE IN YOUR GARDEN DURING LOCKDOWN?

Sharing the screen with Ann-Marie and giving a garden tour to the My Real Garden gang on what was the first official Sunday Social.

WHAT IS THE ONE THING YOU DISCOVERED DURING LOCKDOWN THAT YOU WILL REPEAT?

During lockdown I kept thinking about the families that I work with, who would be staying at home with small children for weeks on end, many of whom wouldn't have access to any outside or green spaces. I discovered how fortunate I was to reap the therapeutic benefits of spending time in my garden.

WHAT PLANT WOULD YOU NOT BE WITHOUT IN YOUR GARDEN?

Tulips, tulips, tulips. Some years, to my shame, I've let my tulip bulbs rot in the shed. Not this year though. I've placed my bulb order early and I'm looking forward to a fabulous display in spring.

> **"The catalyst for beginning a new project was the removal of a tall hedge at the front of the house."**

WHAT (OR WHO) HAS BEEN YOUR MOST UNEXPECTED LOCKDOWN GARDEN VISITOR?

Butterflies and bees. They were drawn in by *Verbena bonariensis* and *Salvia nemorosa* 'Caradonna'.

YOUR GREATEST GARDENING SUCCESS DURING LOCKDOWN?

Finding 'Lady of Shalott' – a shrub rose that will thrive in part shade. This rose has orange scented blooms and is repeat flowerer - what's not to like?

Growing hope

What my garden means to me

@tinaworboys @new.court

Name: Tina Worboys
Location: Ealing, London

morning for a coffee break and we'd all sit in the sun-baked front garden and enjoy the flowers and textures that we'd normally just walk past. We could chat to neighbours and passers-by whilst still feeling secure in our space. The front garden helped make us feel connected in those strange early days when everything was unsettling.

My best memories are of my children and their friends running round, jumping over the trailing plants, climbing up the bench and over the wall. I was so happy with the garden, it hit the spot as an eye-catching feature but more importantly it was loved by the whole family and used as a proper garden, not just an entrance to look at.

> **"We could chat to neighbours and passers-by whilst still feeling secure in our space."**

Front and centre in our lives

Lockdown hit just after we'd decided to leave London. We'd had an offer accepted on a lovely place in the countryside and were ready to leave when everything ground to a halt. Suddenly I was a schoolteacher to my four- and seven-year old. Our one break in the park each day resembled a rubbish episode of One Man and His Dog as I attempted to round my children up without encroaching on anyone else's space. Thank goodness for our gardens (front and back) and our allotment. Spaces to learn, grow and calmly just be a family.

Without our garden, lockdown would have been so different. My husband would stop working mid-

For the first time ever I have made jam - far easier than I thought and definitely the perfect way to use home-grown and hedgerow fruits.

That all important first impression

My unloved front garden was given a cottage look on a budget

@tamsinwesthorpe

Name: Tamsin Westhorpe
Location: Herefordshire, England
#sharingourgardens #gardenlove #myhappyplace #gardeninggirl

The planting has a cottage theme, with roses being a priority. There are lots and lots of pots up the pathway full of herbs, dahlias, edible and annual flowers. My larger back garden has been a football pitch for my son during this time, so here my plants are safe from flying footballs.

Outside the back door is a wonderful table and benches made by a local craftsman from a tree that once lived in the woods I can see from the house. I've spent hours sitting here listening to @myrealgarden and working on my laptop – it's a hot spot for our wifi.

DO YOU GARDEN ALONE?
My husband dislikes gardening but he is wonderful at cutting the back lawn. The front garden is very much my domain. However, I'm pleased to report that my teenage son has been persuaded to help me on occasion throughout lockdown.

WHAT WAS YOUR LOCKDOWN EXPERIENCE?
I usually spend my summer welcoming guests to my family's open garden just up the road. That garden remained closed, so for once I've had time at home to look after my own garden – and I've loved it. It's been refreshing to tend a garden that no one will judge or comment on. This is just for me.

DESCRIBE YOUR GARDEN.
Although I have a garden that's over an acre, I have focused all my attention on my much-ignored small front garden during lockdown. I'm very aware that the front garden offers that all important first impression, and being a garden writer and gardener I feel it has to be up to scratch. My house is ancient, and the front garden also has a few historic features – one being a stone coffin (yes really)! A body was found here many moons ago and the coffin is a registered monument that I now use as a bird bath.

WHY WAS YOUR GARDEN SO IMPORTANT OVER LOCKDOWN?
I have a very active mind but in the garden I'm able to switch off. Pottering around in my front garden has been wonderful therapy. I'm not someone who likes to sit still for long, so it has kept me fit and fulfilled. Without it I'd have been working out with Joe Wicks – so fortunately the family were spared that!

WHAT IS YOUR BEST MEMORY OF YOUR GARDEN?
The day I spotted my husband

#frontgardens

sitting in the front garden listening to @myrealgarden was a memorable one. For someone who professes to hate gardening he was engrossed.

WHAT IS YOUR FAVOURITE GARDENING HACK?

I've been using a cocktail shaker to harvest my seed. Pop a seed head in the shaker, put on the lid, shake and then tip the clean seed into an envelope – genius.

SHARE THE QUIRKIEST THING YOU'VE DONE IN YOUR GARDEN DURING LOCKDOWN?

Sleeping in a tent with my son on one of the windiest nights of the summer. Mind you, being woken by the dawn chorus was amazing. I also regularly enjoy a bit of bat watching at dusk.

WHAT IS THE ONE THING YOU DISCOVERED DURING LOCKDOWN THAT YOU WILL REPEAT?

Using a kitchen fork to prick out seedlings. Saves hours. Also, I have started to paint again. By painting flowers you look at the bloom so closely and it's such a good thing to do whilst listening to gardening podcasts. I also painted a huge wall

frieze for my uncle's garden during lockdown – it's far from perfect but I enjoyed myself.

WHAT IS YOUR TOP RECYCLING IDEA?

To clean the permanent pen off your plastic labels use nail varnish remover, then they can be reused again and again.

WHAT PLANT WOULD YOU NOT BE WITHOUT IN YOUR GARDEN?

Dahlia 'David Howard' – such a wonderfully uplifting plant with colours that give that summery feeling even on a dull day. Love it.

WHAT (OR WHO) HAS BEEN YOUR MOST UNEXPECTED LOCKDOWN GARDEN VISITOR?

Frogs. We've had so many leaping in and out of the coffin this year. On some mornings they've even managed to make their way into the kitchen by slipping under the door.

YOUR GREATEST GARDENING SUCCESS DURING LOCKDOWN?

Buying local. I saved up to have a willow fence made by a local willow weaver. I'm eager that my garden is created using plants and features grown and made locally.

> "I'm pleased to report that my teenage son has been persuaded to help me on occasion throughout lockdown."

I'm passionate about supporting small, local businesses.

HAVE YOU GROWN MORE VEGETABLES DURING LOCKDOWN?
Yes. I've grown lots of potatoes – particularly those that resulted from planting spuds that were sprouting in the veg rack. The best news is that my son has started to eat spinach just because we grew it – success!

Cleome and *Alstroemeria* 'Indian Summer' have provided weeks and weeks of colour in the front garden.

#frontgardens

Growing hope

What our gardens mean to us

@miss_richo

Name: Kath Richardson
Location: Berkshire, England

with little work to do and no human interaction. As an introverted extrovert, lockdown made it difficult to regulate my mood. I suddenly had nothing to juggle, nothing to keep me busy. I felt anxious a lot of the time and struggled to adjust to the lack of routine. The garden gave me back a purpose, a focus for each day. I built my days around spending time in it and it shifted from being something I loved to something I couldn't live without.

On the days when my anxiety was high, I struggled to get myself out and into the main garden, but I knew being outside would help ease my mind, so I started to sit on the front doorstep. Hunkered down at the low level I felt cocooned and hidden from view. Once I was outside I started to potter whilst I was there. Weeding turned into moving pots from the main garden, potting up plants and seedlings from the borders and what emerged was not only a little garden but a way to ease my anxiety.

> **"It shifted from being something I loved to something I couldn't live without."**

A focus for each day

Living in a top floor maisonette, I'm fortunate I have a garden at all, but it's not connected to my house. It is behind the row of terraces and accessed via a shared path from my front door. Being so far from the house, I rely on a water butt to keep things watered so my plants need to learn fast how to survive in arid conditions (whether they like it or not!).

The house is situated on a quiet, no-through road so there's little in the way of traffic – both vehicular and human. As my neighbour isn't a gardener, I commandeered part of her front garden to use as a nursery for my seedlings.

I live by myself and lockdown was spent working from home,

Self-employed and in shock

Both my husband and I are self-employed. I run a cleaning business and he is a relatively recently qualified driving instructor. My business continued at half pace and David's stopped overnight. We were at home with our boys, who are 17 and 18, and my daughter was in London as an occupational therapist in Charing Cross hospital. My elderly parents fortunately live in the same village as us. In March our lovely cat was hit by a car and broke her pelvis, so she had her own lockdown for 12 weeks that ran concurrently with ours.

After the initial shock and numbness, which lasted about a week, we got motivated. We painted, we cleaned, we worked, and we volunteered and shopped a lot for others. We found joy in where we were, in food and in the garden and the sun shone on us.

Discovering @myrealgarden has been wonderful – I learnt so much and I can't wait to put it all into practice next spring and summer. I remember the day I requested to join Ann-Marie on Instagram Live to ask about my pear tree – thanks to her advice I had my first juicy pear.

Strangely we found a peace and strength from it all and the garden benefitted for the extra attention. My mum, who is 84, found her gardening mojo came back again and – at a distance – we shared gardening tips. She now posts pictures on Facebook of her many clematis, and last week her heritage tomato 'Brandywine', which was weighing in at 1lb 3oz!

"My 84-year-old mum found her gardening mojo again."

@joannawinter5453

SEED STARTER SET

Name: Jo Winter
Location: North Devon, England

#frontgardens

Plant a wisteria in your front garden right away! It was the first thing we planted at the front of the house – 19 years later I can't imagine my garden without it.
Mar Fernandez @mar_gardenpassion

Hacks, Tips & Tricks

What makes a welcoming, wow-factor front garden?

A front garden allows you to make friends with gardening neighbours so that you can share surplus seeds and young plants. I can't eat 100 lettuce or plant out 500 apricot foxgloves, but I can swap them!
Vicki Scott @middlelangdoncottages

Afternoon tea can become an event no matter the size of garden (just watch out for garden wildlife that might be rather partial to a slice of cake.)
Dean Halsey @deaninthegarden

Recycle, recycle, recycle. Tubs, cans, tins, small toy trucks, tyres, coconut shells and used water bottles can all be made use of in the garden. You'll save a fortune by making your own compost.
Viharika Parankusham @witch_of_herbs _and_potions

Have confidence in yourself and your garden. Really own it. Do what you want with your space and if you treat it with love and respect, it will reward you.
Julie Savory @juliesavoryneejames

Joan Wright
Think about how you plant your garden to ease maintenance. Flowers amongst low hedges make for a warm welcome home without creating too much work.

Donna Loveday has made great use of her walls for climbing and hanging plants.

CHAPTER 06

Small Spaces

When you garden in a small space such a strong relationship is formed with the plants and features. These gardeners have filled every inch by using inventive design - you won't find bare soil here!

#smallspaces

@breezegardendesign

· · · ·

Name: Sue Creak
Location: West London, England

#inmygarden #hydrangeas

A city sanctuary

Great fun was had sowing out-of-date seeds and wishing then to germinate

DESCRIBE YOUR GARDEN.
It's about 18m long and set on the diagonal, copying the lines of the extension. There are two squares of lawn also on the diagonal, which means larger planting areas on the sides that are triangular so more planting space than having narrow borders along each side. We built a brick path, deck and marked out the lawns and edged it with clay pavers – it was the first garden I designed and a great place to try out plants. The *Euphorbia characias* subsp. *wulfenii* and *Stipa arundinacea* (now called *Anemanthele lessoniana*) have seeded themselves around a lot and add some continuity, as do the box cubes on the corners that I grew from small plants. The garden could really do with a new fence and paving as this would make it look so much smarter. We are very close to the underground & the North Circular, but we are lucky to have lots of trees (mostly sycamore) that filter out the noise and make it feel far more country like than it is. The front garden is tiny, and filled with a curvy box hedge and roses, hydrangeas, grasses and perennials.

WHAT WAS YOUR LOCKDOWN EXPERIENCE?
Normally we are away at weekends a lot, so all these endless weekends at home meant time to tidy up the garden, weed cracks in the paving and plant out-of-date seeds from the shed to see if they grew – at least one from each packet sprouted. I am always on a mission to reduce the things in pots but this made it worse! In hindsight, I would have planted annuals straight into the ground as I think they would have grown faster and stronger.

WHY WAS YOUR GARDEN SO IMPORTANT OVER LOCKDOWN?
Just somewhere to be outside especially with all the fantastic weather. It made me realise how important gardens are, and how we should endeavour to protect them from developers and build more houses and less flats so that people can have their own space. I also realised how important our parks are – walking to Ravenscourt Park to meet a friend for a picnic, I passed so many other parks on the way that I didn't know even existed – full of people enjoying the outdoors.

WHAT IS YOUR BEST MEMORY OF YOUR OWN GARDEN?
Having neighbours around for impromptu drinks after a concert in our road, and my gym friends taking it in turn to visit each other's gardens.

WHAT IS YOUR FAVOURITE GARDENING HACK?
When potting up, put the smaller plant pot inside the bigger one and fill with soil, then you can quickly tip out the small plant and place in the preformed hole in the bigger pot.

WHAT PLANT WOULD YOU NOT BE WITHOUT IN YOUR GARDEN?
I love hydrangeas – floppy 'Annabelle'. I have one in my front garden that I rescued from a garden centre which is white and fades to green and has fantastic foliage.

YOUR GREATEST GARDENING SUCCESS DURING LOCKDOWN?
Tomatoes – three small plants hastily picked up from Waitrose when I was in a very long queue to get in. The beefsteak ones are amazing with the largest weighing 523g.

"We are very close to the tube & the North Circular, but we are lucky to have lots of trees that filter out the noise."

#smallspaces

Growing in beauty every day

I've got gardening fever and I love it

@carolbentleyme

❤ 💬 ✈ ● ● ● ●

Name: Carol Bentley
Location: Somerset, England

#naughtyspends #fizzonfriday
#feedonfriday

DESCRIBE YOUR GARDEN.

My garden is my safe, happy place – it takes my mind off my current personal situation (uncertainty over my house after a relationship separation and the future of my job). Pre-lockdown, the garden was a green box, mostly laid to lawn, bounded by 1.8m beech hedges. But now I've got gardening fever it's growing in beauty every day. I've dug flower beds, which are packed with dancing sunflowers, colourful dahlias and beautiful calendula. There's an avalanche of veg growing in a myriad of upcycled containers situated on the sunniest side of the garden (which also happens to be the path – not so convenient for the postman!) The garden is also a place for Monty the dog to relax in the shade and cool off in his paddling pool; for me to enjoy a glass of wine, or for my family to eat an al fresco lunch on a hot sunny day.

DO YOU GARDEN ALONE?

Monty dog follows me around, and I share seeds and plants with close neighbours.

WHAT WAS YOUR LOCKDOWN EXPERIENCE?

Because of the house situation I'd been wary of doing anything drastic, but on furlough with nothing to do during lockdown I was sick of looking at lawn. Avon bulbs were selling off their RHS Chelsea Flower Show stock, so I thought, right, let's do it, bought a load and burst into action. Usually I'd get plants from my mum, our gardening oracle, but she lives hundreds of miles away and is recovering from cancer treatment. I bought magazines at the supermarket just because they came with free packets of seeds.

WHY WAS YOUR GARDEN SO IMPORTANT OVER LOCKDOWN?

The garden has been my safe, happy place during the madness. It's grounding and helps me draw a veil over the drama that's going on. It takes me out of my head and into my hands. I love arty, creative projects so I've made a willow obelisk – although it's slightly lopsided I'm still pleased with it. The pleasure and sense of de-stressing I get from gardening on a daily basis is amazing. Having a sea of gorgeousness bobbing at your front door, watching the bees, seeing the journey from tiny seed to full grown fruiting plant – it's magical.

WHAT IS YOUR BEST MEMORY OF YOUR OWN GARDEN?

The first evening I went out and harvested a selection of veg all in one go - tomatoes, courgettes, green and purple beans, carrots, radishes, beetroot and mini cucumbers – all grown in small containers. I felt so proud, excited and couldn't wait to eat them.

WHAT IS YOUR FAVOURITE GARDENING TIP?

One from The Oracle (my mum): If you've missed pinching out your tomatoes and the side shoot has got a bit big, once you've pinched it out you can plant it and get a whole new plant. Genius!

Growing from seed has given me a fantastic garden on a budget and the plants have given Monty the dog a place to hide from the sun.

"There's an avalanche of veg growing in a myriad of upcycled containers situated on the sunniest side of the garden."

SHARE THE QUIRKIEST THING YOU'VE DONE IN YOUR GARDEN DURING LOCKDOWN?

The attempted rescue of Barry the bat with a neighbour. He was crawling about in daylight. The bat protection people advised us to put him in a box, and he was gone the next day. I like to think by the time it got dark he'd recuperated enough to join his friends.

WHAT IS THE ONE THING YOU DISCOVERED THAT YOU WILL REPEAT?

Lockdown gardening was a bit like make do and mend – you grew what you could find. Next year I'd like to plan more. I'll repeat growing annuals from seed. It seems like a faff but they look so beautiful.

YOUR TOP RECYCLING IDEA?

Use vitamin tubes to put on the end of canes. (Because every time I use a cane without anything on the end I hear my mother saying, "You'll have your eye out on that.")

WHAT PLANT WOULD YOU NOT BE WITHOUT IN YOUR GARDEN?

Dahlias and sunflowers. I love the richness of the colour and styles. They make such a statement.

WHAT (OR WHO) HAS BEEN YOUR MOST UNEXPECTED LOCKDOWN GARDEN VISITOR?

Limbo toad. A toad was on my compost bag. As I moved the bag he ended up doing the splits. One leg on the bag and another on the hedge.

Growing hope

What my garden means to me

@carolyn_ramsamy

Name: Carolyn Ramsamy
Location: Enfield, London, England

A testing time shielding

Just before lockdown, I'd visited my local nursery and bought all the seeds I would need on the allotment for the year. I'd also bought compost and some growbags. Then I got the letter saying that I must shield. Feeling uncomfortably in touch with my own mortality, and shielding even from my family in the house, I took to the garden – sowing seeds, potting on and moving things. From morn to night, I was outside, with a work bench set up in the garden. I grew and grew. My only meltdown was running out of compost and tonic water the same day!

The garden was where I could feel safe. I started a journal cataloguing what I was growing and counting the days until I could be let out 'on parole'. I slept in the loft away from everyone and danced around them in the kitchen… but outside in the garden I had space and my family and I could comfortably be together. Once a week I would head to the allotment to plant out the veg. I even built a little raised bed at home to grow lettuces and we've not bought any all summer.

> **"I slept in the loft away from everyone and danced around the family to avoid them in the kitchen… but outside in the garden I had space."**

#smallspaces

"This year there has been an unbroken chain of flowers and colour."

Frogs and hedgehogs are regular visitors to our garden and they are most welcome. Providing water certainly attracts the wildlife.

Wild, windy but wonderful

It's an extreme place to garden but over 40 years we've mastered it

@anneski5

Name: Anne Francis
Location: County Durham, England

DESCRIBE YOUR GARDEN.

Our garden is only 10m x 10m and is set about 150m up in the Northern Pennines, on the edge of a rural town. Outbuildings at the bottom of the garden are the last barrier to very strong winds that blow down the dale unhindered for 25 miles. It's an extreme place to create a garden. We have lived here for almost 40 years and the garden has morphed from veg garden to family garden with a lawn, to gravel garden with patio space. It contains two ponds, a small bog garden, flower bed, the gravel garden with a number of containers, amongst which are four trees – a mountain ash and a horse chestnut, a crab apple and a 'James Grieve' apple tree. To save space, we also have step-over apples, which are used as a safety barrier in front of a drop to protect our grandchildren. We have visiting hedgehogs and resident frogs, and our garden is next door to a rookery, so crows, rooks and jackdaws are regular visitors.

WHAT WAS YOUR LOCKDOWN EXPERIENCE?

I returned to growing vegetables and had success with peppers, tomatoes, courgettes, potatoes, and salad crops. We removed the metal grid from the raised ponds knowing the grandchildren wouldn't be around for months. The frogs loved that. The gravel area became smaller and smaller as pots and containers filled the space.

WHAT IS YOUR BEST MEMORY OF YOUR OWN GARDEN?

The plants in my garden that are linked to a memory or person have become ever more special to me. I can link many of the plants to friends and family, past and present. Most plants carry a memory as well as enhancing the garden, some are recent but many are from our first garden or when our daughter was young.

SHARE THE QUIRKIEST THING YOU'VE DONE IN YOUR GARDEN DURING LOCKDOWN?

Watching the bats that live in our outbuildings at dusk has caused great entertainment, as has watching the nightly return of birds to the rookery next door.

WHAT PLANT WOULD YOU NOT BE WITHOUT IN YOUR GARDEN?

I could not live without roses and trees. I also adore the poached egg plant (*Limnathes douglasii*) because it encourages so many hoverflies.

YOUR GREATEST GARDENING SUCCESS DURING LOCKDOWN?

Normally there is a plant lull during July and August. This year there has been an unbroken chain of flowers and colour.

HAVE YOU GROWN MORE VEGETABLES DURING LOCKDOWN?

Yes. Initially so that we had food in case there was a shortage. Everything had to grow in containers and pots that I had available. Peppers, courgettes, tomatoes, salad crops and potatoes were all a great success.

#smallspaces

"One of my most successful lockdown projects was upcycling an old bookshelf into an auricula theatre."

Buzzing bees, birdsong and buckets!

Repurposing vintage items has allowed me to create a unique garden

@darrenlakin2

Name: Darren Larkin
Location: Yorkshire, England

#potager

DESCRIBE YOUR GARDEN.

The garden is my sanctuary. It's a happy mix of cottage garden style borders with a potager vegetable garden. We have lived here for 13 years and spent the first couple of years focusing on the house before moving on to the garden. In our previous home we had just a yard and I had only grown in pots so this was my first proper garden completely made by me. It was originally overgrown, full of things like scrap bikes, and is flanked on both sides by enormous conifers, which creates a challenge. I enjoy looking for inventive methods to upcycle and make features myself. This is something I have always enjoyed so it was great to have a new space to play with.

One of my favourite features is the gazebo seating area, which is filled with comfy botanical cushions and embellished with vintage finds. There's no shortage of pots here! The greenhouse, work yard and cold frame are again places where I have enjoyed adding vintage features.

WHAT WAS YOUR LOCKDOWN EXPERIENCE?

Never before has so much time and continued effort been spent in the garden. I've undertaken everything from seed sowing to maintaining borders and planting pots. One of my most successful lockdown projects was upcycling an old bookshelf into an auricula theatre.

WHY WAS YOUR GARDEN SO IMPORTANT OVER LOCKDOWN?

In a word, sanity. Having the garden has enabled me to spend time outdoors making and creating. This gave me a focus and enabled me to shut out the terrible situation the world found itself in.

WHAT IS YOUR BEST MEMORY OF YOUR OWN GARDEN?

Walking outside early every morning and just sitting in amongst the plants and flowers with my coffee. Being accompanied by the buzzing of bees and birdsong was a great start to every day.

WHAT IS YOUR FAVOURITE GARDENING HACK TO SHARE?

Buckets. Enamel and galvanised buckets make absolutely great planters, be it for bulbs, bedding plants or even vegetables, and seem to work in every style of garden. It's easy to find them in vintage salvage or junk shops – if they have a hole in it's all the better as this allows for good drainage. They are lighter than stone or terracotta pots so can easily be moved around the garden.

SHARE THE QUIRKIEST THING YOU'VE DONE IN YOUR GARDEN DURING LOCKDOWN?

Video-chatting friends who were doing more in their gardens than ever before. They were keen to ask me how to do things and it was great fun showing them how to garden from my own plot. It's been great to have the technology to share my passion for horticulture.

WHAT IS THE ONE THING YOU DISCOVERED DURING LOCKDOWN?

It's not a race. The more time you spend in your garden the better it will be. Patience is a virtue that gardeners must learn.

WHAT IS YOUR TOP UPCYCLE IDEA?

Making your own wooden seed trays out of pallets is easy. I also had fun making herb plant labels

#smallspaces

from scrabble tiles. The source of my 'finds' is absolutely anywhere. I just keep my eyes and mind open to how things can be reused and scour vintage centres, salvage yards, online auction sites, boot sales and charity shops. I think vintage garden ephemera adds charm and a quirkiness to the garden that I like and enjoy.

WHAT (OR WHO) HAS BEEN YOUR MOST UNEXPECTED LOCKDOWN GARDEN VISITOR?
A family of goldfinches that repeatedly visited the garden to drink from a rusty metal rose sculpture that had filled with rainwater.

YOUR GREATEST GARDENING SUCCESS DURING LOCKDOWN?
It was so rewarding sowing seed this spring and summer. Having much more time allowed me to sow far more flowers and vegetables than normal and enjoyed harvests of asparagus, salads and potatoes.

Growing hope

What my garden means to me

@otisthegardener

allowed me to focus on something important that I'm really passionate about. It takes me to another place where I don't have to worry about things. I really enjoy looking after my plants and that it's all down to me to make sure the garden thrives and looks great.

Name: Otis Scadding
Location: Wimborne, Dorset, England

> "I live with anxiety and depression and gardening for myself (and others) has been the best thing to stop me worrying and keep positive."

It takes me to another place

I set up my own gardening and design business two years ago, which I love, and luckily working outside has meant I've been able to carry on throughout lockdown. It's been lovely to work with my clients, although we have not been able to be in the garden at the same time. They have sent me messages or talked through the window if they wanted me to focus on something in particular. I live with anxiety and depression and gardening for myself and others has been the best thing to stop me worrying and keep positive.

   I have good and bad days with my anxiety. Being in my own garden

#smallspaces

My passion and my happy place

The front garden has given me and passersby so much pleasure

@donnajloveday

Name: Donna Loveday
Location: SW London, England

2 DAYS AGO

DESCRIBE YOUR GARDEN.

My garden is a typical, modest-sized London garden bordered by fences and, on one side, a very dominant, white-painted wall. The garden is divided into two zones. There's a lower paved section with a seating and eating area, then there are steps up to a circular lawn with borders around it. I love sculpture so there are a number of small stone busts and plinths located around the garden. The dominant, south-facing wall is now a backdrop for fruit trees and a grape vine that extends all the way across it.

WHAT WAS YOUR LOCKDOWN EXPERIENCE?

Spending so much time at home and in the garden, I wanted to make the time as productive as possible. I am a design curator and wanted to use my skills and experience to reinvigorate the garden. So I conceived a number of small lockdown projects, which included creating a sculpture wall as a backdrop to a seating area; renovating an old bench (found in the loft and destined for the tip) to create a seating area in front of a tree in one corner of the garden; installing a water feature on the patio area; and in the front garden creating a trellis display on a bare wall decorated with objects and planted with my favourite summer flowering plants.

WHY WAS YOUR GARDEN SO IMPORTANT OVER LOCKDOWN?

It has been vital – I'm not sure what I would have done without it. I have so enjoyed working in the garden, listening to birdsong and seeing that the more plants, feeding and water stations I added, the more wildlife came. It has been a solace in such difficult times and given me a much-needed boost during lockdown. It also sparked conversations that would not ordinarily have taken place. People walking past my front garden would stop to say how much pleasure it brought them – we discuss what I'm growing and exchange gardening advice and ideas. What has brought me the most pleasure is to see how, in difficult times, a garden has the power to raise a smile, start a conversation and establish friendships.

FAVOURITE GARDENING ADVICE?

Think about a special place – it could be an exhibition, museum or garden you have visited – and try to recreate something from it in your garden. My sculpture wall was inspired by a visit to the Sir John Soane's Museum in Holborn, London.

WHAT PLANT WOULD YOU NOT BE WITHOUT IN YOUR GARDEN?

I do love plants with lush green foliage and dramatic leaves – banana plants, cannas, *Fatsia japonica* and heucheras have all given amazing displays this year.

YOUR GREATEST GARDENING SUCCESS DURING LOCKDOWN?

Creating focal points in the garden and, through more considered planting, attracting more wildlife. As a result of introducing a number of water stations around the garden, I now have a resident family of frogs.

"A garden has the power to raise a smile, start a conversation and establish friendships."

Placing a bench in the front garden made me use the space more and look at life from a different angle. Growing climbers is a great way of getting the most out of a tight space.

#smallspaces

"It gave me a chance to sort out my little yard, and love it back to life"

Reveling in the silence

I hadn't really appreciated my garden until now

@hilaryfaymellor

Name: Hilary-Fay Mellor
Location: North-west Yorkshire, England

DESCRIBE YOUR GARDEN.

A tiny walled courtyard, behind a small ironstone cottage, facing east and leading off the kitchen. I rent this house so I grow a lot in pots and containers, even larger and woody plants such as acers, bamboos and grasses. There are trees and shrubs in the ground too, and it was very shady, so I have pruned substantially so that now there is light by the house. The garden is at its best in spring with hellebores, prunus, sarcococca, viburnum and camellias bringing early interest. The rest of the year it is a green oasis. There is a seating area by the back door, a little border with an apple tree, a clematis and a weigela by the wall, and an out-of-sight covered area with pots, wheelbarrow and so on. In the sunny section there is an olive tree in a pot, a pallet turned into a green wall, and a hanging basket.

WHAT WAS YOUR LOCKDOWN EXPERIENCE?

Lockdown was spent with my 21-year-old son and two dogs. I am a gardener, so I could still work, although all my design work was put on hold, so I was working to about 40% capacity. I absolutely loved the peace, empty roads, blue sky and silence, and I was so aware of the awesome power of nature during the fabulous spring weather. It gave me a chance to sort out my little yard and love it back to life. Until lockdown, I was very unappreciative of it, wanting a "proper" garden, and using it as a dumping ground for plants for work. I also enjoyed cooking proper meals and having quality time with my son. I also found Instagram (I thought it was like a dating app previously!) and online yoga and meditation.

WHY WAS YOUR GARDEN SO IMPORTANT OVER LOCKDOWN?

I was lucky enough to work outside, so still got out. Some of my clients are elderly, so I was a bit of a lifeline for them. When I went shopping, people's fear and anxiety was visceral. As soon as I got back into the garden, I felt peaceful and grounded and quite joyful. I felt a huge disparity between human energy and the earth's energy.

WHAT IS YOUR BEST MEMORY OF YOUR GARDEN?

Sitting in the garden at dusk, watching the stars appear and reveling in the silence, with just the odd owl hooting - heaven.

WHAT IS YOUR FAVOURITE GARDENING ADVICE?

Dig up your lawn and grow a meadow or herb garden instead.

SHARE THE QUIRKIEST THING YOU'VE DONE IN YOUR GARDEN DURING LOCKDOWN?

Meditation, stargazing and having a lot of conversations with blackbirds that visit the wall trough that's under my window.

WHAT PLANT WOULD YOU NOT BE WITHOUT IN YOUR GARDEN?

Prunus incisa 'Kojo-no-mai'. I planted it in memory of an old dog, and it heralds the start of spring, and brightens up a gloomy day in March.

WHAT (OR WHO) HAS BEEN YOUR MOST UNEXPECTED LOCKDOWN GARDEN VISITOR?

A plague of rats, I was afraid!

#smallspaces

"We had breakfast, dinner and tea in the garden. It was lovely to have a safe sanctuary to sit and relax in."
Mary Whelan
@Mary.whelan.520

"We've watched the swallows arrive and leave, watched foxes, bats, played table tennis, clapped for carers and watched the lightning."
Alison Renyard
@sunflowersbytheseaside

"The garden was somewhere to switch off. I had time to stop, listen and enjoy."
Kim Dalton
@the.clay.gardener

Sunny thoughts

"I've fallen in love with fuchsias. I have about 30 of them in the garden – a number of which I've grown from cuttings."
Lottie Doyle-Edwards
@lottiedoyley

"My garden has been my sanctuary – a place to create, a place to ponder and a place to just be."
Lindsay Henderson
@Lindsaythegardener

"I grow mainly succulents and air purifying plants – they come in all shapes and sizes and add such interest to my home."
Rachel Cherryholme
@cherrybomb.73

"I adore hydrangeas but they don't love my soil so I plant them all in large pots which I place in the garden beds."
Fleur Beckwith
@fleurbeckwith

"The more time I spend in the garden, the happier I am and the nicer I am to others."
Shobha Vanchiswar
@seedsofdesignllc

Growing hope

What my garden means to me

@ilse.vanoosterhout

♥ 💬 ✈ • • • •

Name: Ilse Vanoosterhout
Location: Belgium

2 DAYS AGO

New job – new passion

I started my new job on 1 March 2020 as a nurse specialising in 'prevention and protecting people at work'. Two weeks later, we went into lockdown in Belgium. It was a stressful time for me. Instead of the normal activities at work, everything involved Covid-19. I neglected my garden during the months of March, April and May, as when I came home in the evening, I was just too tired to do anything in the garden.

It was halfway through May, when I planted my dahlias, that I found the energy to do some gardening. At that time, I discovered @myrealgarden. It inspired me to grow annual flowers. I even wanted to grow some vegetables. Working a 40-hour week,

I started small. I bought five young tomato plants, I sowed radishes and some salad.

I'm a real flower girl at heart – I love flowers and the butterflies, the bees and bumblebees that visit them. I sowed tagetes, cosmos, zinnias, nasturiums and sunflowers. As everything started to grow, I spent more time in my garden after work and still do so to this day.

My garden was my safe place, where I didn't have to think about Covid-19. It gives me joy and happiness to see something growing from seed or a bulb. Gardening is really important for my mental and physical health and it always helps me through difficult times.

> "Gardening is really important for my mental and physical health - it always helps me through difficult times."

Name: Kate McGorty
Location: Grantham, England

#higgledy

Housework has taken second fiddle to gardening

DESCRIBE YOUR GARDEN.
My garden was originally the yard of a Victorian terrace house, with lovely old walls on two sides. It's made up of concrete slabs and shallow borders, so a lot of planting is in containers of various types. Every inch of space is used, with planters hanging from the fencing and baskets put up wherever the opportunity allows. At the far end of the garden I have placed a table and chairs as it's a suntrap there in the later afternoon. There is a mature buddleja against the wall that fills the air with scent and attracts the butterflies on a sunny day. Over the back wall are old laburnum and lilac trees. My variegated jasmine and a clematis have borrowed these to climb through, and as a result the jasmine is the height of a tree. I suspect that the mature ivy is holding the wall together – my feathered friends adore it.

DO YOU GARDEN ALONE?
It's my garden but I shout for help and don't climb steps! My granddaughter loves to investigate my plants when she visits.

WHY WAS YOUR GARDEN SO IMPORTANT OVER LOCKDOWN?
Sanity. Having the garden stopped me from overdoing the dreaded housework. I also have an allotment too, which gave me a great excuse during lockdown to go for a walk.

WHAT IS YOUR BEST MEMORY OF YOUR OWN GARDEN?
I was thrilled when the sun-loving agapanthus that I grew from seed a few years ago flowered for the very first time. I also enjoyed getting my compost from the milkman!

FAVOURITE GARDENING ADVICE YOU'D LIKE TO SHARE?
Send off for seed catalogues. Nothing beats flicking through the pages and writing lists of all the plants you plan to grow or dream of growing.

WHAT IS THE ONE THING YOU DISCOVERED DURING LOCKDOWN THAT YOU WILL REPEAT?
That there are no rules when it comes to gardening. There is more than one way of doing things and we should all go with our instincts.

WHAT IS YOUR TOP RECYCLING TIP?
Making paper pots out of old newspaper and using them for seedlings is such a great idea. You can also save a fortune by making use of anything that will hold compost as a pot. I'm also a firm believer in giving any surplus plants away – you never know, you might encourage someone to take up gardening just by giving them a few spare seedlings.

WHAT (OR WHO) HAS BEEN YOUR MOST UNEXPECTED LOCKDOWN GARDEN VISITOR?
I was thrilled to discover Mr Toad. He was a very well behaved and welcome guest.

YOUR GREATEST GARDENING SUCCESS DURING LOCKDOWN?
I grew the most enormous tomatoes. The variety was 'Noire de Crimmee', commonly known as Black Krim. This tomato has incredible flavour, goes almost black when ripe and is very juicy. My largest tomato weighed in at an impressive 485g.

"Every inch of space is used, with planters hanging from the fencing and baskets put up wherever the opportunity allows."

#smallspaces

"The garden gave our days structure as we settled into a rhythm."

Growing my own edibles has been so rewarding. My plan was to grow the veg that was hard to find in the shops and I succeeded.

The garden was our world

My little boy has grown into a gardener

@Bumblebeesandbluebells •••

Name: Mieke Philips
Location: Cambridge, England

#inmygardentoday #wildlifegardening

DESCRIBE YOUR GARDEN.

I have a small, long, city centre garden in Cambridge where rain is scarce. As space is limited, I have hardly any lawn and grow both vertically and horizontally. I often have Vita Sackville-West's mantra in my head: "Cram, cram, cram, in every nook and cranny".

The garden consists of three parts: a flower garden, a wildlife garden and a kitchen garden. I try to create lots of habitats by planting climbers, leaving heaps of branches and planting shrubs and ground cover to provide safe places and hideaways. Thanks to the dense planting and the layer of mulch I apply every autumn, weeds do not get much chance but there are several bedding pockets amongst the perennials filled with annuals, tender perennials and bulbs. These change twice a year and are propagated in my greenhouse.

WHAT WAS YOUR LOCKDOWN EXPERIENCE?

Inspired by Aaron Bertelsen at Great Dixter, I decided to grow a lot more food in containers. I grew all the vegetables from seed, and pricking out seedlings has become one of my favourite activities. For months on end, the garden was our world. My son would nap under the apple tree or I'd be sitting quietly as the day drew to a close, listening and feeling part of this beautiful world. As the seasons progressed, it reminded me of the impermanence of this situation. Plants and wildlife just went on with their business and that gave me a sense of security and connection.

WHAT IS YOUR BEST MEMORY OF YOUR OWN GARDEN?

Witnessing my son grow and enjoy the garden. He has changed a lot during lockdown and grew into a confident, delightful and aware little person. He loves spotting bees and blackbirds. He saw me getting ready to start planting seedlings a while ago and handed me my trowel!

WHAT IS YOUR FAVOURITE GARDENING ADVICE?

Invest in good, peat-free compost and get seeds from small companies.

Good quality compost means your germination rate increases hugely and your seedlings get off to a good start as they develop good root systems. Smaller companies often have seeds from unusual or heirloom varieties, which taste gorgeous.

SHARE THE QUIRKIEST THING YOU'VE DONE IN YOUR GARDEN DURING LOCKDOWN?

Sitting quietly in the garden when it is getting dark and listening to the life in the undergrowth and watching the bats and the stars come out. I even saw a shooting star one evening.

WHAT IS YOUR TOP RECYCLING IDEA?

Grow tomatoes in reused compost bags. You gain more growing space for free, and if you put nice pots in front of them, you won't even notice the bags.

HAVE YOU GROWN MORE VEGETABLES DURING LOCKDOWN?

Definitely. I enjoy growing vegetables you cannot buy and that hold memories of travels or family abroad, like courgette 'Fiorentino'. My son loves cucumbers and is half Turkish, so I grow a Turkish cucumber called 'Cengelkoy'. I also grew two types of aubergines and had a generous harvest before October.

#smallspaces

Hacks, Tips & Tricks

When space is limited ideas can still be big

Make room for spring. Tulips, narcissi, aquilegia and forget-me-nots were the stars of the show and gave me so much joy.
Lisa Downing
@lisamdowning

@victoriajaynesgarden

Victoria Atkinson
Sweet peas and cosmos last for ages in a vase (or a milk bottle!) and plants will repeat flower after picking.

A tall coldframe to grow seeds with my kids has been brilliant.
Alex Warren
@leafy_alex

Painting your fences black expands space in a small garden, and plants look great in front of it too.
Esther Dobbin
@ramblings_from_north

When I feel overwhelmed, I deadhead. It totally relaxes me, I feel accomplished, and it's a certain way of getting more flowers.
Rene Johnson
@pb_williams

Take as many cuttings as you can, from your own garden, but from friends, neighbours and family too. Plants for free – easy.
Gwendoline Doyle
@doyle1910

@partridgerita

Rita Partridge
Even in the smallest garden, hidden areas tucked under trees will allow you to attract the wildlife.

Hot colours and giant foliage
give a garden that holiday vibe

CHAPTER 07

Tropical Retreats

What could be better than transforming your garden into a retreat that reminds
you of far-flung places? These gardeners have embraced dramatic foliage
and flowers to create paradise on the doorstep.

#tropicalretreats

A newfound sense of connection

I never feel I am gardening alone as I'm part of many planty communities

@thechigardener

Name: Darren Kench
Location: Birmingham, West Midland, England
#boyswithplants

DESCRIBE YOUR GARDEN.

When I inherited my own 1930s suburban garden, back in 2006, other than a patchy lawn and a neglected shrubby border, the only discernible feature was a shed, which was dwarfed by a large silver fir. The fir tree dominates the garden, providing a dramatic focal point that overshadows all else, so I employed the use of a Japanese pagoda as a secondary focal point. This echoes the tree's pyramid-shaped canopy, drawing the eye down and through the garden. The pagoda became the springboard for a Japanese-themed water garden. A trip to the Kyoto Garden in London's Holland Park fuelled this obsession with water and inspired me to create a pond.

Over the years, my palette of plants has become more diverse. I've been creating a foliage garden of lush, architectural planting, punctuated by exotic flowers and pollinator-friendly plants. A bespoke trellis screen and archway combine to form a grotto behind the pond, from where you can access a secluded wildlife-friendly garden. Here, you'll find *Dryopteris filix-mas* (male fern) hugging the silver fir, beyond which an L-shaped meadow wraps around a bug hotel, crowned with a green roof.

DO YOU GARDEN ALONE?

Although I live alone, I never feel like I'm gardening alone. I belong to many gardening communities, who I share my passion with, be that on Instagram or through the voluntary work that I do for Leasowes Walled Garden in Halesowen and several local gardening groups.

WHAT WAS YOUR LOCKDOWN EXPERIENCE?

Just before the country went into lockdown, I presented with mild symptoms of coronavirus and was required to self-isolate. After self-isolating I returned to my place of work as a graphic designer in the display industry, covering for furloughed staff and supplying much of the country's Covid-19-related display and signage solutions. During this time, I decided to launch the 'Plant a Thought' project, growing and distributing free sunflowers, to coincide with Mental Health Awareness Week and to encourage people to plant for pollinators.

WHY WAS YOUR GARDEN SO IMPORTANT OVER LOCKDOWN?

As a result of the reduced socialising we've all had to get used to, and the extra time it's afforded me, I've discovered a newfound sense of connection with my garden and the wildlife I've been privileged enough to share it with, not to mention the wonderful @myrealgarden community.

SHARE THE QUIRKIEST THING YOU'VE DONE IN YOUR GARDEN DURING LOCKDOWN?

After only three days of being housebound, I assembled and squeezed myself into a cold frame to illustrate a gardener's experience of self-isolation, which became a 'meme' that I titled 'When a gardener needs to self-isolate.' It didn't break the internet, but it made me laugh!

#tropicalretreats

> **"I've discovered that vegetables can be just as beautiful as flowers, and often more bountiful."**

WHAT IS THE ONE THING YOU DISCOVERED DURING LOCKDOWN THAT YOU WILL REPEAT?

Prior to lockdown, I'd never really been much of a vegetable gardener, mainly because I don't have a lot of available space left to grow vegetables, but growing space-saving varieties, vertically, has changed all that. I've discovered that vegetables can be just as beautiful as flowers, and often more bountiful, so they'll definitely be making a repeat appearance in my garden.

WHAT IS YOUR TOP UPCYCLING IDEA?

During lockdown I converted a clear storage box into a hedgehog feeding station, with great success, thanks to a tip-off from hedgehog guardian @hals_urban_hedgehogs on Instagram. I've also created an insect house out of a repurposed wine bottle box. The latter is a good excuse to pop a cork or two!

WHAT PLANT WOULD YOU NOT BE WITHOUT IN YOUR GARDEN?

Iris sibirica 'Tropic Night' grows in abundance in my garden. Its striking violet-blue flowers emerge in May and are held aloft slender, grassy foliage, which adds textural interest long after the flowers have faded. They make good pond marginals, but the largest clump I have is happy in clay soil, and the other is contained in a pot.

WHAT (OR WHO) HAS BEEN YOUR MOST UNEXPECTED LOCKDOWN GARDEN VISITOR?

One evening, after realising I'd left my shed unlocked, I ventured outside and heard a rustling in the border. To my delight, I discovered a hedgehog had paid a visit. I registered my sighting on www.hedgehogstreet.org and built a feeding station to encourage their presence. Hedgehogs should have water left out for them and they enjoy meaty cat and dog food. I'm so thrilled that my garden is hedgehog friendly.

YOUR GREATEST GARDENING SUCCESS DURING LOCKDOWN?

My French climbing beans have given me the most satisfaction and reward for my effort. Growing low-maintenance, high-yield varieties that you love is a sure-fire way to success.

Growing hope

What my garden means to me

@butterfliesinthegreenhouse

Name: Claire Gilder
Location: Cheshire, England

and blessed that we are lucky enough to have this outdoor space. It's vitally important for mental and physical well-being. The garden has definitely been the thing that has kept me going throughout the lockdown when I couldn't see my closest family due to working in the hospital and the tropical look I have created has definitely given me that much needed holiday feel.

"Long shifts during the pandemic have been testing at times."

On the front line

I have been on the front line for the NHS during this pandemic so have not been furloughed, working full-time in masks for 12-hour shifts, so the garden has been an absolute sanctuary to come home to. During lockdown we created a Japanese area in the garden on my days off for relaxation. I wanted a space that reminded me of being in a garden spa that we once visited, and I'm thrilled that we managed to pull it off.

Long shifts in the NHS during the pandemic have been testing at times and very tiring. Whilst I work with an amazing team and we have all supported each other, being able to return in daylight to a beautiful garden has been a godsend. I feel so fortunate

#tropicalretreats

A family who never felt cooped up

@aprilhousegardens

Name: Emily Crowley-Wroe
Location: Gloucester, England

#plantsmakepeoplehappy

DESCRIBE YOUR GARDEN.
Our backyard has been transformed into an outdoor garden room, giving the family extra space at a crucial time. It's an open, flexible space used for relaxing, exercise, dining, play, sleepovers, sky-gazing, bat-watching, drinks, dancing and growing as many exotic-looking plants as possible. We wanted to be transported to some far-flung place the moment we stepped into the garden. We choose contemporary double-slatted panels to increase privacy and planted in front of these in borders on the ground and in large, raised containers. Most of the garden is decked so that it feels like an indoor room extending from our narrow living/dinning room. Little seating nooks can be found amongst the raised planters in between huge banana plants, as well as a hanging swing seat from a corner pergola perfect for sky gazing and snoozing. A pond in one of the raised containers is full of aquatic plants so that we can hear the resting sound of water and to attract wildlife. In the front garden we used old pallets for a pop-up veg patch, planted beech hedging to screen an old fence and provide a wildlife habitat and made a bed for the kids to grow plants from seed.

DO YOU GARDEN ALONE?
The garden is mainly my domain but during lockdown the kids enjoyed growing veg and my non-gardening husband even made the raised beds out of pallets for the front garden.

WHAT WAS YOUR LOCKDOWN EXPERIENCE?
The garden quite literally saved us. My husband was diagnosed with cancer, my first show garden at RHS Malvern was cancelled and my new business venture came to a halt, and the kids were lost without friends and school. Every night we'd sit outside watching the bats, toasting marshmallows and being very thankful for such a wonderful space and being together in it when all was chaos outside. During the day I lost myself in wheeling tonnes of soil from the front to the back, planting up the garden, which was landscaped just as lockdown came, and planting veg and seeds with the kids out the front.

WHY WAS YOUR GARDEN SO IMPORTANT OVER LOCKDOWN?
The constant stream of alarming news, the general feeling of fear and helplessness about Covid-19 and my husband's cancer diagnosis was tempered, and at times escapable, because of the focus on planting and improving the spaces for our family. We never really felt cooped up because of the garden and the amazing weather at the time.

WHAT IS YOUR BEST MEMORY OF YOUR GARDEN?
Sometime in May, one evening the four of us snuggled on the swing seat reading *Clever Polly and the Stupid Wolf* out loud and watching the bats swooping overhead after toasting marshmallows on the fire pit.

WHAT IS YOUR FAVOURITE GARDENING HACK?
Virginia creeper (*Parthenocissus quinquefolia*) gets a bad press but I keep mine for the jungle vibe I'm

The decking has allowed us to run in and out of the house bare foot and it's made a great surface for summer garden games.

#tropicalretreats

> **"We wanted to be transported to some far-flung place the moment we stepped into the garden."**

after. I keep the long vines, strip the leaves and use them to make wreaths at Christmas time.

SHARE THE QUIRKIEST THING YOU'VE DONE IN YOUR GARDEN DURING LOCKDOWN?
The kids used the pale deck boards to finger paint pictures using water.

WHAT IS THE ONE THING YOU DISCOVERED DURING LOCKDOWN THAT YOU WILL REPEAT?
To spend some time every evening outside watching the sky, hearing the birds and walking around (wine in hand!) really seeing the plants and all the subtle nuances in their growth and decay.

WHAT IS YOUR TOP IDEA FOR REUSE OR RECYCLING?
Gather dead leaves in the autumn and stuff them in bin bags with air holes to make your own leaf mould.

WHAT PLANT WOULD YOU NOT BE WITHOUT IN YOUR GARDEN?
Goat willow tree (*Salix caprea*) provides shelter over the swing seat, canes for propping up plants, captures dandelion seeds from the fields in its catkins and houses birds and insects.

WHAT (OR WHO) HAS BEEN YOUR MOST UNEXPECTED LOCKDOWN GARDEN VISITOR?
The biggest dragonfly I have ever seen - an Emperor I think - has visited several times, and we've had lots of common frogs in the ponds.

YOUR GREATEST GARDENING SUCCESS DURING LOCKDOWN?
Planting up the entire back garden room and seeing it realised from a paper plan to a flourishing, exotic-feeling jungle.

HAVE YOU GROWN MORE VEGETABLES DURING LOCKDOWN?
Previously I've never felt I had the time to grow them, so lockdown encouraged me to give it a go. The biggest thrill were the pumpkins and sweetcorns. This year we will cook the pumpkins rather than carve and waste them.

I filled my world with colour

Embracing clashing colours makes for a brighter and happier scene

@thedistinctivegardener

Name: Nick Gough
Location: London, England

#happygardeninglife #gardenideas
#sundayvibes #inmygardentoday

DESCRIBE YOUR GARDEN.

In 2014, on the agent's viewing day, it was the garden I had come to see. It did not disappoint. Though neglected and overgrown, it immediately cast a spell over me. We secured the house, builders set to work on the house and I set to work on the garden. There I discovered a plaque that said the garden had been designed, built and loved by one couple, George and Marjorie Carter, for over 68 years. It was time to restore it to its former glory.

My garden is several gardens rolled into one and on three different levels. There is the cottage, gravel, woodland and water garden, as well as the circular terrace. There are cosy corners, secluded seating areas and views and vistas from the many benches that are dotted here there and everywhere. I love plants, so my garden is full of them in all shapes, sizes and colours. It is a place to share, a place to reflect, a place to be close to nature and most importantly, the people I love. My real garden is me.

DO YOU GARDEN ALONE?

I suppose the garden is my domain, but Elena loves the garden too. And I think at least two of my teenage kids have been seen in it at least once a year.

WHAT WAS YOUR LOCKDOWN EXPERIENCE?

23rd March 2020: blue skies, blossom, tulips and fear. We were

told to stay at home and that is what we did. For those fortunate enough, we stayed in our gardens too. Living in London, the silence was at times hard to contemplate. No cars, no aeroplanes, no people on the streets. It was both wonderful and frightening all at the same time. As a garden designer, meetings with clients about their new gardens were now held on computer screens. This was a wonderful distraction we all found solace in. If we can grow and create there is hope.

WHY WAS YOUR GARDEN SO IMPORTANT OVER LOCKDOWN?

My garden was a sanctuary, a place where I felt all my family could escape to and feel safe. A place to relax, a place to have fun in, a place to marvel at the wonders of nature. A place to gather our thoughts and, through gardening, look ahead to a safer future.

WHAT IS YOUR BEST MEMORY OF YOUR GARDEN?

So many. The stillness, the blossom, the cleaner air, the birdsong. Nature taking over once again. The wonder of sowing free seeds from a magazine and watching them grow into wonderful flowers.

#tropicalretreats

WHAT IS YOUR FAVOURITE GARDENING ADVICE?

If you like it, grow it! Throw whatever you like together – who cares if the colours clash? Create your own colour palette and enjoy it! If you fill your world with colour your world will always be a better place.

SHARE THE QUIRKIEST THING YOU'VE DONE IN YOUR GARDEN DURING LOCKDOWN?

Planting up old saucepans and baking dishes that my late mother once cooked in with succulents . A wonderful way to be reminded of the ones you love on a daily basis.

WHAT IS THE ONE THING YOU DISCOVERED DURING LOCKDOWN THAT YOU WILL REPEAT?

To live in the moment. To take time to look, really look!

WHAT IS YOUR TOP RECYCLING TIP?

Water tanks. Whenever you see a loft conversion skip, check if there is an old metal water tank being thrown out. They make amazing planters and look fantastic.

WHAT PLANT WOULD YOU NOT BE WITHOUT IN YOUR GARDEN?

Cannas. From the moment the fantastic foliage appears, you know you are in the presence of greatness. Then comes the long buds and the flowers!

WHAT (OR WHO) HAS BEEN YOUR MOST UNEXPECTED LOCKDOWN GARDEN VISITOR?

My teenage children!

YOUR GREATEST GARDENING SUCCESS DURING LOCKDOWN?

Dahlias in pots. Everywhere, all over the garden they offered big, bold and brassy flowers. Fabulous.

HAVE YOU GROWN MORE VEGETABLES DURING LOCKDOWN?

Yes. Pick-again salad, rocket and strawberries. It all tasted so much more delicious than anything bought from the shop.

"The silence was at times hard to contemplate. No cars, no aeroplanes, no people on the streets."

#tropicalretreats

Growing hope

What my garden means to me

@greengoldgardensgh

Name: Rosaline Nutsugah
Location: Accra, Ghana

Growing a new business

On 27th April 2020, I decided that it was now or never! Covid-19 had taught me that nothing was assured and that we needed to live fully in the present while demonstrating love to our neighbours. I realised with stark clarity that I had to live my passion right then. I started on the first steps of my long-awaited journey by developing 'Green Gold Gardens' a garden centre which is open to the public and serves as a green space. I call it "My Slice of Paradise."

Since I started on my garden centre journey, not only have I met some amazing people and grown in so many ways, but I have also made great sales! A variety of plants, garden accessories such as planters, plastic and terracotta pots, wrought iron planters and pot stands, as well as outdoor garden furniture are all on offer. All these accessories are locally manufactured because collaboration is a key part of my vision and encouraging local artisans is an integral part of Green Gold Gardens' ethos.

This has been an incredible journey and acquiring knowledge about plants whilst simultaneously having fun is really important to me. In the New Year, I look forward to starting a series of workshops in the garden, such as kokedama (moss-ball) wrapping sessions, macrame-making classes and pot-painting parties - all with Covid-19 protocols observed, of course - some of which I will host and others which will be delivered by other entrepreneurs. I wouldn't change my new "Green Gold" life for anything.

> **"I started on the first steps of my long-awaited journey by developing a garden centre."**

Hacks, Tips & Tricks

For a truly tropical slice of garden paradise

Love my *Canna* 'Musifolia' – the ultimate exotic plant. It's made even more gigantic by feeding it with my very own alpaca fertiliser!
Lou Archer @louatlarches

@bella.lyingdownmum

Ros Robertson
Mature, large-leaved plants like our tetrapanex brings welcome shade. We're trying to get ours to colonise the rest of the garden!

Make a cabinet of curiosities by painting an old shelf unit with fence paint. Everything in mine has a special memory.
Liz Cooper @allmyown73

To make sure you get great cut flowers, cover your dahlia tubers in sand. When they come into growth slugs are deterred. Works for me.
Debbie Mitchell @debbiemitchell65

Tree ferns prefer rain water, so I've bought a rainwater butt and have been collecting rain from the garden shed roof with buckets and watering cans.
John Lyons @john_and_his_fronds

Extreme heat and lack of water this lockdown summer made me rethink new planting to be more drought resistant – exotic plants are the perfect solution.
Dawn Evans @dawnevansgarden

@elaineportch @williamportch

Elaine & William Portch
Gardens are important extensions to your living space, a place to be creative in and a place to enjoy daily so make yours your own – and sit and appreciate it from time to time.

Jo Gallon has created a comfy
corner in her Leeds garden

CHAPTER 08

Town & City

The aim of every urban gardener is to transform their plot into a place where they can escape the hustle and bustle of a busy environment. These gardeners have achieved that in spades.

"We were excited when ducks arrived but quickly discovered how disruptive they are – they ate everything."

© Rik Pennington

I'm a proud career changer

The garden has been my playground and sanctuary during lockdown

@clancycatherine

Name: Catherine Clancy
Location: Greenwich, England

DESCRIBE YOUR GARDEN.

We moved here two years ago, so it's a relatively new garden. This city plot is a sharp contrast to the garden of my childhood in Ireland, which was huge and surrounded by countryside. However, this garden is much bigger than my last plot, which was a courtyard behind a terraced house, and now I have side access & parking (luxury). I gave up my allotment when we moved here, as my current garden is big enough to grow fruit & veg, and has a greenhouse.

Before we started work it was a horrible empty, dark wasteland, but it had so much potential. There was not much growing in it except a few scruffy shrubs, weeds, and a massive dying *Cupressus macrocarpa* (Monterey cypress). As a garden designer I know all too well the many challenges that people face when creating a city garden but I love designing small gardens –

every centimetre counts, and you have to be creative for the garden to have big impact. This is my sanctuary, my playground, and although I had a rough plan for the layout, I am largely making it up as I go along. I've tried to reuse what was already there in the old garden, like the old sandstone paving, which is not lovely, but absolutely fine.

DO YOU GARDEN ALONE?

I mostly garden alone but my husband cuts the lawn. I share the garden with friends and family and I grow plants for them, particularly veg plants. Over lockdown I have encouraged so many others to grow their own veg.

WHY HAS YOUR GARDEN BEEN SO IMPORTANT OVER LOCKDOWN?

My studio window overlooks the garden, which is such a privilege. I'm proud to say that I am a career changer – once an IT manager and now a gardener. I started my garden design business in 2005, after taking part in Diarmuid Gavin's *Garden School*, filmed by the BBC, based at RHS Wisley. The outdoor space has been a godsend – to have social distanced client meetings outside has been invaluable.

WHAT IS YOUR BEST MEMORY OF YOUR GARDEN?

Finding newts in the pond. I've never had a pond before and didn't really know what I was doing when I made it, but it's such a joy to find creatures such as frogs and water snails just arriving in the pond of their own accord. Provide water and a suitable habitat and they will appear. We were excited when ducks arrived too – but quickly discovered how disruptive they are! They ate everything, and we had to resort to netting the pond.

WHAT IS YOUR FAVOURITE GARDENING ADVICE?

However small your garden is there is no excuse not to grow veg or herbs. Grow what your like to eat in pots – it's such a joy.

WHAT PLANT WOULD YOU NOT BE WITHOUT IN YOUR GARDEN?

I have adored my salvias, *Clematis viticella*, herbs and of course roses.

HAVE YOU GROWN MORE VEGETABLES DURING LOCKDOWN?

I haven't grown any more veg than usual, but I have got others into growing more. I've grown veg for years and now have a patch at the end of the garden. I love homegrown salad, potatoes, corn, tomatoes, beans, herbs... grow what you like to eat.

#town&city

My garden has never looked so good

@mike_thegardener

...

Name: Mike Palmer
Location: Bournemouth, Dorset, England

#shareyourgarden #inmygarden

DESCRIBE YOUR GARDEN.

I designed and planted our L-shaped back garden two and a half years ago. It's a strong, geometric design based around three circular lawns and a circular, grey, limestone patio that houses a garden office. The design is softened by dense, RHS Chelsea Flower Show-type planting with structure being provided by acers, tree ferns, ornamental pears, Indian bean trees and a stunning *Cercis* 'Forest Pansy'.

I'm a real plantsman and I adore my perennials. The garden is crammed with lavenders, geraniums, penstemons, astrantias and geums, amongst many others. These beautiful perennials jostle cheek by jowl around roses, grasses and evergreen shrubs, including *Skimmia*

x confusa 'Kew Green'.

In spring, fifteen to twenty containers are crammed with three different tulip varieties that flower from March until May. Once the tulips have finished their performance they are replaced with home-grown *Cosmos* 'Dazzler' and a selection of stunning dahlias, most of which are pollinator-friendly, single flowered varieties, including *Dahlia* 'Bishop of Auckland'.

I love strong, contrasting colours in my garden; dark burgundies, bright oranges, deep purples and sizzling reds all sing out from the generous borders. Winter interest is provided by hellebores, drifts of snowdrops and the beautifully scented winter box.

DO YOU GARDEN ALONE?

I garden largely alone, as Director of Gardening. My partner provides invaluable help as Director of Everything Else!

WHAT WAS YOUR LOCKDOWN EXPERIENCE?

On Friday 27th March, I nervously hit the 'Live' button on Instagram and proceeded to wander somewhat aimlessly around my garden with a captive audience of FOUR. My 'Weekly Wander' continued every Friday throughout lockdown, but week 10 saw me chatting live with

the lovely Ann-Marie Powell in her garden, and what a laugh we had. Since then, I've chatted to a number of lovely people in the gardening world live on Instagram, all thanks to Ann-Marie and @myrealgarden. There is a fantastic gardening community out there on social media. I have always found gardeners to be extraordinarily generous with their time and knowledge and lockdown reinforced this belief. I have made some real (albeit currently virtual) friendships within this community.

WHY HAS YOUR GARDEN BEEN SO IMPORTANT OVER LOCKDOWN?

My garden has always been my sanctuary, but during lockdown, more so than ever before it became my place of normality amid the madness of Covid-19 and my haven away from the horrifying statistics. I spent hour upon hour sowing seeds, dividing perennials, weeding until not a weed was left and mowing until not a blade of grass was bent out of shape. I planned, re-planned, moved plants around and (thankfully) bought more plants from our fantastic online plant retailers.

WHAT IS YOUR BEST MEMORY OF YOUR OWN GARDEN?

Plants were lined up, ready to be planted before the garden was finished. As I thrust my spade into

Being so close to the sea the garden benefits from a mild climate that's perfect for tropical plants

"To my horror, 13 tonnes of bricks had been pushed into the garden when the old house on our plot was pulled down years earlier."

the soil a loud 'clang' rang out. To my horror, 13 tonnes of bricks had been pushed into the garden when the old house on our plot was pulled down years earlier.

WHAT IS YOUR FAVOURITE GARDENING ADVICE?

I've always used the adage 'a pound on the soil and a penny on the plant'. If our plants are to thrive, treat them to a healthy well-conditioned soil.

WHAT IS YOUR TOP RECYCLING TIP?

Use, re-use and re-use again all plastics until they literally cannot be used again.

WHAT PLANT WOULD YOU NOT BE WITHOUT IN YOUR GARDEN?

Astrantias have a very special place both in my heart and more importantly in my garden.

WHAT (OR WHO) HAS BEEN YOUR MOST UNEXPECTED LOCKDOWN GARDEN VISITOR?

Most unexpectedly one Friday morning, as I was doing my Live Weekly Wander, who should walk through the garden gate but the one and only Tamsin Westhorpe (garden writer), armed with plants.

HAVE YOU GROWN MORE VEGETABLES DURING LOCKDOWN?

Sadly, no. It's all about the flowers... and 6 tomato plants!

Growing hope

What my garden means to me

@feecameronlondon

Name: Fee Cameron
Location: Charlton, England

work from home. The dining table became my desk with its view down the garden. @myrealgarden lunchtimes became a joy, listening to and learning from wonderful people, sharing our community's passion for gardening.

Throughout, the garden was my calm, my oasis, grounding me in the positivity of nature when news of the virus was consuming us all. It balanced the stresses of commuting and the day. I guess it was mindfulness at play: focusing on the little things, watching the tiny daily changes during my morning and evening mooches around the garden, checking in with my lockdown spot on the planet, and with myself. @myrealgarden gave me the opportunity to share the time with some inspiring people and to learn more about gardening.

> **"Commuting by train was stressful so I dusted off the old bicycle."**

London is a world away

I chose to live here because of the long, 24m garden that runs behind the Victorian terrace. The living room window looks down the garden and all you can see is plants and sky. It is remarkably peaceful away from the street at the front. You can close the door and London is a world away. Then, at the end of March 2020, I changed jobs at 24-hours' notice to support the key organisations delivering London's Covid-19 response. It was humbling, working with the capital's best in such challenging times. Initially, I worked in London Fire Brigade's HQ in Southwark. Commuting by train was stressful so I dusted off the old bicycle. After a while, I could mostly

@secretgardens

Name: Jo Gallon
Location: Leeds, England

My recovery garden

DESCRIBE YOUR GARDEN.

We moved into our new-build house in autumn 2019 – it had a wraparound garden with about 50 metres of the dreaded builder's fence and newly laid turf. The back of the garden has an easterly aspect onto a field that we have access to. We decided to break the space up into a series of rooms to make it more manageable. One of these would be a courtyard garden with no grass, a space for us to all relax and sit together or entertain friends round the fire pit. We wanted it to have a slightly chic contemporary feel, with cottage garden planting. Our aim was that it would remind us of our favourite holidays in Provence and Cornwall. There are two huge, raised beds planted with beautiful herbaceous plants including veronicastrum, scabiosa, lots of different salvias and geraniums. We've had to screen one of the fences with pleached hornbeam but although they are quite formal the blousy *Hydrangea paniculata* in baskets underneath them really relax the whole feel – there are such a lot of lovely plants and fantastic foliage to enjoy.

DO YOU GARDEN ALONE?

I garden with my husband Andy, and the children Millie and Teddy help with seed sowing, deadheading and watering.

WHAT WAS YOUR LOCKDOWN EXPERIENCE?

On 21st March 2020 I came down with Covid-19 symptoms. A couple of weeks later I was still in bed, but I discovered @myrealgarden. It was a life-changing moment. I was still quite poorly so I don't remember much about that time other than watching the Instagram Lives Ann-Marie did every day. It became a huge distraction to my situation. No matter how poorly I felt, I was determined my new-build garden journey was about to begin.

Unfortunately, it took me nearly 5 months to recover. While I was in bed, I spent time ordering plants, seed and compost. Within a month or so I was able to be outside for a short time and start sowing seeds then potting on – planting out – feeding – watering – and before I knew it nearly 5 months on I have a real garden. I call it my recovery garden!

WHY WAS YOUR GARDEN SO IMPORTANT OVER LOCKDOWN?

Being unwell with a disease that the medics didn't fully understand yet was a frightening experience, and despite my hugely positive outlook I did feel at times quite scared back in March. With a garden there is always hope. I've gardened in fits and starts over the years but spending more time outside healed me. As time went on, I felt able to start planning the bigger things we needed to do in the garden and became stronger. The days became longer and warmer, the garden centres opened, and the naughty spends began! Having access to this space has made realise how lucky I really am.

SHARE THE QUIRKIEST THING YOU'VE DONE IN YOUR GARDEN DURING LOCKDOWN?

I don't think there's much we haven't done in the garden during lockdown. Laughed, cried, eaten, drunk, grown, feasted, played and a whole lot of watering! The craziest thing we did was buy a house built on a former quarry. We spent days using a pickaxe to excavate holes in the

> "No matter how poorly I felt my new-build garden journey was about to begin."

bedrock for the 5 pleached hornbeams.

WHAT IS THE ONE THING YOU DISCOVERED DURING LOCKDOWN THAT YOU WILL REPEAT?
Feeding Friday. I use a whole bottle of seaweed feed every week now.

WHAT PLANT WOULD YOU NOT BE WITHOUT IN YOUR GARDEN?
Rosa 'Gentle Hermione'. Wow, if you don't have this rose yet you should! She is the most delicate blush pink, old-fashioned rose with exquisite petal formation. She flowers prolifically twice, and you won't find a stronger sweet-smelling rose.

WHAT (OR WHO) HAS BEEN YOUR MOST UNEXPECTED LOCKDOWN GARDEN VISITOR?
Two deer peering over the fence. We have also had visits from a pheasant, heron, red kite, nuthatch, frogs and lots of butterflies.

YOUR GREATEST GARDENING SUCCESS DURING LOCKDOWN?
I think it's got to be the things we grew from seed – sweet peas, nigella (love-in-a-mist), tomatoes and salad crops.

Hugged by plants

The garden was the perfect place for hide and seek and bug hunts

@growingintolandscape

Name: Gillian Davies
Location: Bristol, England

2 DAYS AGO

DESCRIBE YOUR GARDEN.

From a typical Victorian terrace back yard in the city of Bristol we have carved out a densely planted gravel garden. Over the last two and a half years the space has been brought to life with planting and wildlife; a huge contrast to the paved-over ground that was here when we moved in. Although a small family garden, I was intent on packing plants into the space and creating places for our little boy, Rowan, to play amongst them. Luckily, Rowan is impressed with having so much gravel to dig in. He is absolutely thrilled to have little hide-outs formed by tall grasses and perennials. A retaining wall built from upright sleepers was designed to double up as balancing steps and create a curved hidey-hole. I had decided that instead of having a clear open space as a young child's play area, I would create a space that was packed with sensory interest (this was mainly my justification for being able to buy plants!). It's paying off as we all love a bug-hunt, but Rowan is especially confident amongst his slugs and woodlice.

DO YOU GARDEN ALONE?

I am the gardener, Rowan does the digging and my partner Paul gets called in for the big jobs. Shameful, I know, but I'd rather plant a border than paint a fence.

WHAT WAS YOUR LOCKDOWN EXPERIENCE?

Lockdown was a shock to the system, of course. Paul started to work from the spare bedroom, and I embarked on the daunting task of keeping a three-year-old entertained at home. Missing my mum and friends was the hardest part, as they really are the grounding force when negotiating with a young child becomes almost too much to bear. Simultaneously, an overwhelming feeling of thankfulness and sadness all wrapped up together was so powerful at that time; knowing what others were going through and imagining what was to come was emotional overload.

WHY WAS YOUR GARDEN SO IMPORTANT OVER LOCKDOWN?

There is no doubt in my mind that if this had happened at any other time of year, I would have found it so much harder. As it became clear that the world was retreating indoors, my garden was showing signs of growth. Daffodils started to show up and the allium foliage was lush and promising. I lived in the garden. Noticing growth and new life was more powerful than ever before. The garden's life-force was never to be scrutinised so closely again and that feeling never to be forgotten.

WHAT IS YOUR BEST MEMORY OF YOUR GARDEN?

Sneaking into the garden at 6.50am and sitting still for twenty minutes. Two blackbirds, and an unidentified third bird, hopped along the fences and picked at the ivy. It doesn't sound like much, but without the usual traffic buzz, three birds and some early spring sunshine was absolutely magical.

#town&city

FAVOURITE GARDENING TIP YOU'D LIKE TO SHARE?

I recommend planning seating areas to anyone creating a garden Sitting with privacy from neighbouring windows, enveloped by planting is what dreams are made of in a city garden. Creating new spaces to nestle garden chairs was one of my lockdown tasks; I wanted to feel hugged by the plants.

WHAT PLANT WOULD YOU NOT BE WITHOUT IN YOUR GARDEN?

Calamagrostis x *acutiflora* 'Karl Foerster'. It adds valuable height but is light and airy. Standing strong throughout winter it provides a slight vale of mystery as to what's beyond. And I can't get enough of seed heads; the house is filled with dust-laden arrangements. Hang them upside down until dry and you'll have your spring garden joy throughout winter.

WHAT (OR WHO) HAS BEEN YOUR MOST UNEXPECTED LOCKDOWN GARDEN VISITOR?

Not strictly a visitor because it stayed, but I impulse bought a crab apple tree to match one we already had. A 3m tree, dragged through the house, blossom and all!

HAVE YOU GROWN MORE VEGETABLES DURING LOCKDOWN?

It's the first time I've grown more than strawberries – we've had tomatoes, cucumbers, radish (that the caterpillars got more from) mangetout and rocket. We started it to engage Rowan, but I've loved it more.

"Sitting with privacy from neighbouring windows, enveloped by planting is what dreams are made of in a city garden!"

Lockdown forced us to press pause

We used to go to the gym for stress relief and exercise but now we garden

@maketheworldabeautifulplace

Name: Shane Eason & Jac Blanco
Location: Detroit, Michigan, USA

#feedingfriday

DESCRIBE YOUR GARDEN.

Our garden sits on a half-acre plot of land and our house dates back to 1921. This garden has seen many keen gardeners in its history, most notably its previous owner, Richard Serlin. Local newspaper articles from 1971 stated that he held a giveaway of over 500 plants upon selling the house, and another stated that he had outrageous amounts of bulbs: some 2,500 tulips and 1,500 daffodils.

When we purchased the house in 2016, however, what we inherited was a skeleton of Serlin's design. The property consists of a front garden, an east-facing garden with a pergola, and a conservatory. We renovated the front garden with the key focus of echoing the symmetrical architecture of our house and it has successfully woven formality and informality together with plantings of evergreens to give winter interest and structure along with loose perennials to give pollinator interest and colour. It also allows us to converse and exchange tips with neighbours, so we never feel alone when in that space. Our conservatory allows us to get a head start during Michigan's fickle spring season. With the exciting reinstatement of the pergola, we now have a horticultural golden opportunity in being able to establish separate garden rooms in the east-facing pergola garden.

WHAT WAS YOUR LOCKDOWN EXPERIENCE?

Prior to lockdown, we both led incredibly busy lives, and it felt at times that we always had something going on. Lockdown forced us to press the pause button on that style of life. During this period, we have had more time to reflect on what is important to the both of us: some things are similar, and others are different, but we both immersed ourselves into horticulture. We began to become a bit obsessed with collecting various gardening books, and we even decided to enrol in a garden design distance course at the English Gardening School.

WHY WAS YOUR GARDEN SO IMPORTANT OVER LOCKDOWN?

We both really missed going to the gym as we would use this time for stress relief. Our garden replaced it and became that outlet that allowed us to escape from all the problems of the world. Within our garden, there is always something to do, something to learn about, something to experiment with, and something to look forward to.

ANY GARDENING ADVICE YOU'D LIKE TO SHARE?

Wait a full growing season in a new garden to see what you have before making any major design changes.

SHARE THE QUIRKIEST THING YOU'VE DONE IN YOUR GARDEN DURING LOCKDOWN?

Our home is a bit of an anomaly in the neighbourhood as it is one of the only homes with an extensive front porch. During lockdown, we have used the front porch to dine, take naps, and have a nosey as to what neighbours are doing from a safe distance.

WHAT IS THE ONE THING YOU DISCOVERED THAT YOU WILL REPEAT?

Growing from seed has been such a rewarding experience for us. Prior to lockdown, we never felt that we had the time, but after this year it is something that we want to continue.

#town&city

"We began to become a bit obsessed with collecting various gardening books, and we even decided to enrol in a garden design distance course at the English Gardening School."

WHAT IS YOUR TOP RECYCLING IDEA?
We inherited a dumping ground when moving into our house but we have been able to repurpose bricks for edging along borders, re-establish statuary and we have used broken concrete to build a quirky, dry-stacked wall to outline a vegetable patch.

WHAT PLANT WOULD YOU NOT BE WITHOUT IN YOUR GARDEN?
Perovskia. The bees adore it, it adds winter interest to the garden, and it gives a dreamy effect during the summer with its height and purple wispy haze of flowers.

WHAT (OR WHO) HAS BEEN YOUR MOST UNEXPECTED LOCKDOWN GARDEN VISITOR?
We have had a few visits from a hummingbird during lockdown. It would frequently fly into the conservatory to enjoy our tropical hibiscus.

YOUR GREATEST GARDENING SUCCESS DURING LOCKDOWN?
We reinstated the 18m long pergola that was originally built with the house in 1921. It's a thrill to have it back in time for the house's centennial celebration.

Use every scrap of space for plants, mixing it up with annuals from seed, vegetables, herbs and wildflowers. It'll make you feel good and the wildlife will also be very happy.

Yukie Hanada @yukiepring

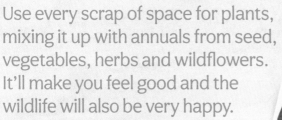

@scottspencer1971buddah

❤ 💬 ➤   ● ● ● ●   🔖

Scott Spencer
Enjoy gardening! I don't think you really learn unless you relax about making mistakes. And sometimes happy accidents make for beautiful gardens.

Hacks, Tips & Tricks

For smart solutions in urban environments

Get a spray lance for watering. It clips into your hose, making it much easier to get into the middle of borders or hard-to-reach containers.

Juliet Holgate @julietholgate

Jo Winter
Every garden should have a firepit – perfect to relax beside after a heavy day of gardening.

Do a little every day. Pull that weed up as you walk out to hang the washing.
Jennie Ewing @_leopardspot

I leave my trowels and hand forks outside in a stone alpine trough for when I fancy a quick weed as you wander.
Teresa Chaplow @teresachaplow

A large garden table can double up as a potting bench and allows for endless alfresco family meals, surrounded by seedlings, plants, sweetly scented air and the buzz of bees.
Shweta Mehta @garden_stories_

Growing annuals like zinnia, cosmos and tomatoes from seed is so exciting. It's a joy to watch them germinate and grow.
Michelle Corbett @mimscorbs

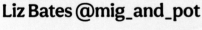

Have a go at some of your own hard landscaping projects. We used recycled materials and I mixed my own cement. The mortar wasn't perfect but I was happy with the results.
Liz Bates @mig_and_pot

···

@tracyjerham

Tracy Jerham
You can grow plants in containers anywhere. Cocooned amongst my collection of plants, I'm in my own hideaway.

Michael Perry's sunny windowsill was an ever-changing display through lockdown.

CHAPTER 09

Containers & Indoors

Everything will grow in a pot given the right care. These gardeners show that,
whether growing inside or out, container gardening opens up endless possibilities.

Nana Min's garden is home to my poultry. The hens were a great hit when the garden was featured on *Gardeners' World*.

The garden forces you to carry on

Experimenting with pots and pampering my poultry has kept my mind occupied

@arthurparkinson_

❤ 💬 ✈   • • • • •   🔖

Name: Arthur Parkinson
Location: Nottingham, England

#gardeningmatters

DESCRIBE YOUR GARDEN.

I have two gardens in my life, one is for pots and one is for poultry, yet neither are properly mine! My mother's garden, Mill Yard, is nothing more than a stamp-sized long rectangle that forms the stage for a path of pots; an array of oval tin baths, dolly tubs and old metal dustbins. They are lined up from the pavement to the front door and their purpose is to provide floral curtains from spring until the autumn. These are planted seasonally with bulbs each autumn, mostly tulips, and then with summer come the annuals – sweet peas, cosmos, panicum grass, sunflowers and dahlias. The selections are ever changing. I love trying new varieties, but the colours are always of stained glass, rich and vibrant tones with flowers that are popular with bees always in mind. Then, up the road, in my Nana Min's long garden, I keep my hens, where they can flap and peck about under the apple trees. Over the past few years, this garden has become rewilded (to give it an 'in vogue' excuse), going from manicured vegetable beds to perennial flower meadow.

DO YOU GARDEN ALONE?

Mostly alone. Nana Min comments at the weeds whilst my mum worries about how much it has all cost. The hens are often around my feet – and occasionally on my head and shoulders too!

WHAT WAS YOUR LOCKDOWN EXPERIENCE?

All my work stopped, and I moved in with my Nana Min as we were worried about her catching Covid-19 via the many carers who were visiting her each day. So I lived with her for 14 weeks from the end of March. This was a precious time, looking after her and making her feel loved. My dad (Min's son) dropped us shopping off each day and we would talk in the garden; for the first time the lockdown gave me my dad's company on a consistent basis. We healed and became friends after being at odds with one another since my early teens.

It was still sort of a busy time as I was writing a book, but I really struggled to write well and get the chapters done. "Oh, I'll do it tomorrow" kept being said in my head and the deadline loomed.

Then *Gardeners' World* rang and asked if I could film the tulips at Mill Yard for their television show with my camera. The hens, most notably Claudia, behaved well and were a hit with the viewers. The Beeb were very impressed with the quality of the film footage, so much so that Mr Don introduced the piece as if the *Gardeners' World* team had actually visited to film.

WHY WAS YOUR GARDEN SO IMPORTANT OVER LOCKDOWN?

It's always been important. It forces you to carry on, it needs as much nurturing as you can give it and gives back in its growth and health. The garden responds to love. Min's garden is important as I wouldn't be able to keep many (or any!) hens if I did not have that. Mill Yard has

183

#containers&indoors

become very much my crazed, flowerpot identity; being a small space, people love it because they can identify with it.

WHAT IS YOUR BEST MEMORY OF YOUR OWN GARDEN?

Sunbathing and getting Min into the garden to pick redcurrants. The hens hatched endless chicks, the parrot tulips were superb as the dry spring meant they were not ruined, and Instagram became a place to talk and meet gardeners.

WHAT IS YOUR FAVOURITE GARDENING HACK?

Cut out photos of plants you're considering for a bed from a plant catalogue and do a decoupage with them to see if they all look good together. Always think about foliage as well as the flowers.

SHARE THE QUIRKIEST THING YOU'VE DONE IN YOUR GARDEN DURING LOCKDOWN?

Muttering to myself – I do it more and more.

WHAT IS THE ONE THING YOU DISCOVERED DURING LOCKDOWN THAT YOU WILL REPEAT?

Not getting too stressed over the garden. I've been a bit more relaxed and stopped treating the front garden like it's a window display in Liberty.

WHAT PLANT WOULD YOU NOT BE WITHOUT IN YOUR GARDEN?

Tulips, a total addiction and craving. *Tulipa* 'Palmyra' was a favourite during this lockdown spring thanks to its dark cherry liqueur red flowers. I adore the stalwarts 'Queen of Night', 'Ballerina' and 'Prinses Irene'.

"The BBC were very impressed with the quality of the film footage, so much so that Monty Don introduced the piece as if the Gardeners' World team had actually visited to film."

WHAT (OR WHO) HAS BEEN YOUR MOST UNEXPECTED LOCKDOWN GARDEN VISITOR?

A beautiful hedgehog both at Min's and, more recently, at Mill Yard too. They are getting rarer due to busy roads and more fences rather than hedges, but also due to a lack of watering holes. Always have a terracotta saucer filled with water in a garden at ground level for wildlife.

HAVE YOU GROWN MORE VEGETABLES DURING LOCKDOWN?

Yes, squash 'Turk's Turban'. I planted these in Min's garden,

digging out a section of the lawn and filling it with rotted hen manure. They won't be eaten, instead they will be still life ornaments inside until they go soft!

Growing hope

What my garden means to me

@grannypattyk

Name: Pat Kinch
Location: Warkworth, Ontario, Canada

new garden for the west side of my house and am now waiting for the hardscaping to completed. It was much better for me to think about plant choices than all the fears of the pandemic.

My grandmother and mother were both skilled gardeners and that gene seemed to have passed me by and jumped to Kat, but thanks to @myrealgarden my own interest was awakened. I found myself mulching, digging and weeding instead of averting my eyes from the hell patch that had developed.

> **"Why would I want to watch a British gardening show at 7:30 in the morning?"**

A wake-up call

My daughter Kat discovered @myrealgarden at the beginning of lockdown and suggested I took a look. There was some delay ("Why would I want to watch a British gardening show at 7:30 in the morning?") but when I finally checked it out I was immediately hooked and only missed two of the Instagram Lives after that. I looked forward to it when I woke up and it started my day with a smile –what lockdown?

I was inspired to see what others accomplished in their lockdown time and was amazed by the before and after pictures, especially of @thisgreencity, @maketheworld abeautifulplace and @birdhouse_ and_bench. I started planning my

Balcony of butterflies and bees

My balcony receives extremes of weather but nothing was going to stop me gardening

@ellenmarygardening

Name: Ellen Mary
Location: Charlotte, North Carolina, USA

DESCRIBE YOUR GARDEN.

My US garden is a small balcony on the top floor of an urban apartment block. It is completely exposed to the elements, from 100 degrees in full sun to tornados and torrential rain in a matter of minutes

Everything is in containers and a Vegepod (a purpose-made veg planter with cover) including salads, vegetables, plants for pollinators, the most gorgeously fragranced jasmine and an abundance of kale, which seems to like the weather here.

Most containers are standing on trays to make watering easier, so the apartment below doesn't end up with the run-off.

Enjoying a gin and tonic in the evenings, as the sun sets over the mountains, listening to the city birds, remains one of my top lockdown memories.

WHAT WAS YOUR LOCKDOWN EXPERIENCE?

I'm a garden podcaster and writer so it was vital that I made the most of the space I had to continue my work. During lockdown I was mostly in North Carolina, as this is where my husband's work takes us. Not able to be in my own garden in Norwich in the UK, or down my beloved allotment, was so tough, but my little balcony here became my mindful haven. It allowed me to have a project, to still be surrounded by plants and get my hands dirty, plus I could try different varieties of plants more suitable to the NC weather. It was an absolute joy watching a concrete balcony come to life.

WHAT IS YOUR BEST MEMORY OF YOUR SPACE?

The first bee that found the lavender was a momentous moment. The balcony is so high up but there it was, buzzing about. That was a very happy day. From then we welcomed birds and butterflies to our little haven.

WHAT IS YOUR FAVOURITE GARDENING HACK/TIP/ADVICE YOU'D LIKE TO SHARE?

Never be restricted by space. A windowsill, balcony, patio, anywhere at all – there is always a plant to grow. If you have no outside space, then houseplants add that real feel-good factor to a room.

SHARE THE QUIRKIEST THING YOU'VE DONE DURING LOCKDOWN?

Watching a tornado was just about the craziest experience – and then realising if we didn't get all of the plants inside quickly, they might disappear! Fortunately, we did get them all to safety in time. I also needed to get creative with flowers inside, so I decided to 'floralise' fun items I had in the apartment. Making flowery sunglasses, bracelets with foliage, hair clips and bow ties was great therapy and also easy for others to do, so I posted the videos on social media to make people smile. It was also great to be able to record Zoom interviews for the Plant Based Podcast to continue spreading the love of gardening.

YOUR GREATEST GARDENING SUCCESS DURING LOCKDOWN?

I grew *Phaseolus vulgaris* – apparently found in a Mexican cave, sealed in a clay pot from 1,500 years ago. They are known as 1,500-year-old cave bean.

"Watching a tornado was just about the craziest experience and then realising if we didn't get all of the plants inside quickly, they might disappear!"

#containers&indoors

"Rocket is a perfect gardener's dog and just wants to be with you. If he can sunbathe, he's really happy."

Having a garden table is vital for potting on, eating out and vases of flowers.

A moveable feast

@lizrentzsch_

Name: Liz Rentzsch
Location: Northwood, Middlesex, England

DESCRIBE YOUR GARDEN.

My garden is a classic Victorian terrace garden, west-facing with a small patio. Measuring about 10m x 5m, it's small but full. I have two small cupboards to grow seeds and start plants off, which have been in constant use this summer. I love pots as you can move things around and change things up in a small garden. My friends call me the Pot Queen as I have so many. Thanks to all the additional plants in pots I have grown this year the garden is now packed with wildlife.

I started renting the house 7 years ago and the garden was empty. Despite being a gardener and garden designer, it's terrible to admit but

I didn't ever plan the garden – it has just evolved. It's overgrown and wild but I like it that way. An important part of my garden is the table. I dress it differently throughout the seasons with vases of flowers and pots of plants. This table is everything – it's where I eat and where I pot things up. Everyone should make room for a table/work bench in their garden.

DO YOU GARDEN ALONE?

I garden alone but I always have my dog by my side. The garden and my dog Rocket have got me through 2020. There is no doubt I would have gone mad without either of them. Rocket is a perfect gardener's dog and just wants to be with you; if he can sunbathe, he's really happy.

WHY WAS YOUR GARDEN SO IMPORTANT OVER LOCKDOWN?

Gardening through this strange time has kept me sane. Planning and sowing was an escape from the news and talking to friends about what we were all doing in our own gardens was my community. It was a total escape.

WHAT IS YOUR BEST MEMORY OF YOUR GARDEN?

Feeding the roses in pyjamas whilst drinking wine. I also adored growing things I had never grown before. Watching all my seeds germinate was a highlight.

WHAT IS YOUR TOP UPCYCLING IDEA?

Plant up any pot – use vintage jugs, vases and old tins and put them in the garden on the table. You don't need to buy new garden pots as there are so many things that can be reused instead.

WHAT PLANT WOULD YOU NOT BE WITHOUT IN YOUR GARDEN?

Roses – I'm addicted to them. I grow over 30 varieties in my small garden, mostly in pots. My top two are the coral 'Boscobel' for her magnificent scent and 'Darcey Bussell' for her crimson-pink colour and non-stop flowers. Both are brilliant as cut flowers, lasting well in a vase.

YOUR GREATEST GARDENING SUCCESS DURING LOCKDOWN?

Growing fruit and veg. I didn't think I could before as I only have a small garden but now, I know it's all possible, even if you only have pots. I have never grown tomatoes before, and until now I didn't understand why people got so excited about them but now I totally get it. I think I will grow them every year from now on.

HAVE YOU GROWN MORE VEGETABLES DURING LOCKDOWN?

I hadn't grown vegetables before. I began sowing as lockdown started, more for something to do than anything else. I'm so glad I did as the rewards have been wonderful and tasty and growing them in pots has worked really well for me.

#containers&indoors

@matt.pottage

Name: Matthew Pottage
Location: Fulham, London, England

No room to swing a cat!

The London micro-climate has allowed me to grow houseplants outside

DESCRIBE YOUR GARDEN.

Eccentric and quirky with a surprising range of plants that you wouldn't expect to see growing outdoors, made possible by the London micro-climate. I'm the Curator of RHS Wisley, so my entire life revolves around plants and my garden is mostly created in containers. Small is my passion! I achieve a sense of depth and space by staging pots on other upturned pots, old crates, and anything else I can get my hands on. Houseplants are important to me and I use them to link the house and garden. A variegated monstera lives by an inside window that looks out to the garden and it works in partnership with the foliage of the trachycarpus in the garden beyond.

WHAT WAS YOUR LOCKDOWN EXPERIENCE?

I suddenly had all my weekends free so found myself in my own garden more and realised, despite how small my space is, I could add a second water feature and MORE plants. I continued to work at RHS Wisley – it was a strange time, as office work and emails almost evaporated overnight, enabling me to get out into the garden and help the team with day-to-day gardening, which was actually really thrilling. I lost weight, got a tan, and my hair went rather blonde on top which caused endless mockery that I'd dyed my hair!

WHY WAS YOUR GARDEN SO IMPORTANT OVER LOCKDOWN?

I live to garden, so no real change for me, but I was so pleased to see friends and family all turning to gardening projects. So many people enjoyed eating meals outside during lockdown, but my garden is so packed with plants that it is almost physically impossible to fit outside with a plate of food. However, I did love the garden on a summer's evening, glass of wine in hand, admiring the plants.

WHAT IS YOUR FAVOURITE GARDENING ADVICE YOU'D LIKE TO SHARE?

With the right amount of water and liquid food, you can do EVERYTHING in pots.

SHARE THE QUIRKIEST THING YOU'VE DONE IN YOUR GARDEN DURING LOCKDOWN?

Taming my neighbour's cat, Gingertail, as I needed some animal contact, and photographing her. I've since put her on my Instagram, got to know the neighbour who owns her, and learnt that she is actually a he called Whale!

WHAT IS THE ONE THING YOU DISCOVERED DURING LOCKDOWN THAT YOU WILL REPEAT?

Walking locally. I've discovered all manner of cool trees and plants in other people's front gardens like *Araucaria heterophylla* (Norfolk Island pine) and bougainvillea.

When it comes to my own garden, I have done more with *Begonia rex*, which perform excellently outdoors as a summer container plant. I've used cultivars with pink and red in them to thread through the wider pot display.

WHAT PLANT WOULD YOU NOT BE WITHOUT IN YOUR GARDEN?

Edgeworthia chrysantha (shown right centre) - how do you get through winter without this plant once you get to know it? It's just something else. The lightly fragrant yellow flowers that appear in late winter and early spring are just sensational.

I don't have room in my garden for many shrubs but I've enjoyed them in other people's garden as I take a walk. The paper bush (left) with yellow balls of flowers is my favourite find.

"I lost weight, got a tan, and my hair went rather blond on top, which caused endless mockery that I'd dyed my hair!"

Keys to a Passion

Growing hope

What my garden means to me

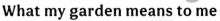

@her_soil_highness

...

Name: Mollie Bowen
Location: Bristol, England

Gardening gave me confidence

When lockdown began, I thought that I'd have the opportunity to finish all those jobs on the list inside the house. However, it became quite clear that time spent in the garden was hugely important for my mental health. The anxiety of being kept apart from family and friends, and fears of what was happening in the world, were helped hugely by spending time in nature and nurturing plants in my own space. The situation was like nothing any of us had experienced before and the anxieties around it were impossible to ignore. For months, each day was the same, at home, but my mood was unpredictable. Some days I'd be motivated to do lots and other days I'd struggle to get dressed. Getting out into the garden gave me purpose. Those plants needed me! As soon as I got lost in a gardening task, a massive weight was lifted. I also set up an Instagram account based purely on my gardening experiences, which introduced me to a supportive and inspiring plant community all around the world. This social network helped me learn, gain confidence, and most importantly made me laugh.

> "The situation is like nothing any of us has experienced before and the anxieties around this are impossible to ignore."

"Once I found my gardening family on Instagram suddenly there weren't enough hours in the day! I planted seeds, potted on, fed and chopped alongside everyone else."
Ailsa Burton @ailsaburton

"I've got my binoculars on my desk and am keeping a log of the insects, birds and animals that visit the garden."
Helen Mason @helly_mai

"I took delivery of a much longed for greenhouse, so I was finally able to grow much more from seed."
Jill Rutherford @jillyrut

Sunny thoughts

"Watching things grow and change with a greater sense of mindfulness was hugely satisfying."
Claudia Pearce @claudia.pearce.5

"I got up in the morning and automatically put on my gardening clothes with my mental to-do list buzzing around in my head."
Jo Hopkins @jhgardendesign

"We took time to sit, relax and enjoy the garden and I suggest you do the same."
Gael Cherry @gael-cherry-design

"Seeing Ann-Marie sowing out of date seeds inspired me to get my old seeds out of the cupboard to see what would grow."
Susan Felton @Susie_222

"I joined Instagram. Wow, all those beautiful plant pictures! I got very inspired."
Eveline Aregger @areggereveline

"Having a windowsill was a good prelude to having my own small garden."

A world on the windowsill

@mr_plantgeek

Name: Michael Perry
Location: Windsor, England

DESCRIBE YOUR GARDEN.

I was staying in an apartment during lockdown, where I experimented with a lovely sunny windowsill, growing all sorts of edible flowers, herbs, a few chillies and even a couple of hardy perennials (such as dicentra). I also played with some solar lights. I truly created an indoor garden, which kept changing and evolving.

WHAT WAS YOUR LOCKDOWN EXPERIENCE?

Circumstance meant I was caught 'on the road' when lockdown hit, as I had been of no fixed abode for a few years, travelling non-stop. It wasn't exactly the right time to stay with friends or rent a new Airbnb. So,

delightfully stuck in Windsor, I filled the apartment with my passion for plants. After four years without being able to, I was ready to grow something. Having a windowsill was a good prelude to having my own small garden.

WHAT IS YOUR BEST MEMORY OF YOUR GARDEN?

The colours, the shapes and textures. It was such a cheerful display, with lots of interest, and a few surprises.

Another great memory of this time was joining Ann-Marie on a @myrealgarden Live on Instagram. Although we work in the same industry, and passed each other at various flower shows and events, Ann-Marie and I have never spent much time together. It's amazing how the internet has actually opened up so many opportunities.

WHAT IS YOUR FAVOURITE GARDENING ADVICE YOU'D LIKE TO SHARE?

Just experiment – try things the text books don't tell you. Follow your instincts. Plants are like people: they aren't all the same, and certainly don't all behave the same.

If you've never grown houseplants before then start with the easy spider plant – you can't fail. However, I would recommend a twist on the usual, with the curly foliage variety 'Bonnie'.

SHARE THE QUIRKIEST THING YOU'VE DONE IN YOUR GARDEN DURING LOCKDOWN?

Growing houseplants upside down! Boskke have designed these unique containers so plants can be grown upside down and the result is really fun. They're very secure and easy to water and care for. I loved de-caning my orchids and suspending them in this way. It's much closer to their natural habitat that way.

Another very quirky thing I did was to hurriedly buy a house during lockdown. I've now moved in and I really couldn't resist giving the garden a makeover. I can't wait for next spring to see how it develops.

WHAT IS THE ONE THING YOU DISCOVERED DURING LOCKDOWN THAT YOU WILL REPEAT?

Short-term, fun displays indoors – I even made a garden on a plate.

YOUR GREATEST GARDENING SUCCESS DURING LOCKDOWN?

I made many orchids very happy! They really have been the stars of the show – they're much underrated.

HAVE YOU GROWN MORE VEGETABLES DURING LOCKDOWN?

Yes, for fun and interest mostly, and to try differences in flavour – I was not imagining I could ever be self-sufficient from a windowsill!

#containers&indoors

No space to plant courgettes in the ground? Grow in a trough. Many courgettes and great architecture...
Rebecca Richards

Piotr Ashwin-Siejkowski
Style your garden to revisit holiday memories; you can then breakfast in Spain, lunch in France, and have supper in Marrakesh.

Hacks, Tips & Tricks

For the ultimate in small-space, big-impact growing spaces

I keep pots on the drive and display them in the garden as they come into flower. Grow in recycled plastic pots and slot them in and out of more expensive display pots.
Jill Rutherford @jillyrut

Growing vegetables from seed is easier than you think in raised beds and containers.
Val Jones-Hughes @valjoho

My garden is an old farmyard, hard-paved. I have a vast selection of containers and my garden layout really is different each year – it's always exciting.
Sally Wicks @sals.garden

Use every container you can find, drilling holes for drainage.
Lucy Allen @lally210

@dustshoveller

Caroline Shenton
Use polystyrene packaging in the base of containers. It provides drainage, keeps the pots light and easier to lift and prevents is going to landfill.

Eve Kerrigan has made the most of a sunny spot by growing agapanthus and sunflowers.

CHAPTER 10

New Gardens

Whether you are new to gardening, have a new plot or have given
a garden a different look - a fresh start is always uplifting.

#newgardens

"It is so exciting to grow things from nothing and then to eat them."

My mum let me watch Instagram to get ideas

I've learnt so much this summer and I can't wait to do it all again

Name: Tom Gilpin
Location: Somerset, England

DESCRIBE YOUR GARDEN.

We haven't got a very big garden and before lockdown it was very messy and had a lot of weird plants everywhere. When everyone was getting worried about food supplies in March there was lots of talk about planting vegetables at home, like during the Second World War and the 'Dig for Victory' campaign. At the time I was studying WWII during homeschool and so I decided to try and grow things to eat too. I didn't think my parents would let me change anything in the garden because we are only renting this house and probably shouldn't dig anything up – but there was a small patch at the top of the garden.

WHAT WAS YOUR LOCKDOWN EXPERIENCE?

I didn't know anything before I started so had to learn what to do as I went along. This proved to be harder than I thought, but after some top tips from various family members I sort of got the hang of it. I'm not old enough to be allowed an Instagram account, but my mum let me watch @myrealgarden sometimes to get ideas too.

WHY WAS YOUR GARDEN SO IMPORTANT OVER LOCKDOWN?

The garden was important because I needed to grow food. I planted tomatoes, peas, lettuce, runner beans, carrots and strawberries. I also grew some flowers too, such as mini sunflowers and sweet peas. Our upstairs neighbour is a retired art teacher but now she loves to make tapestries using a Japanese weaving technique. She was on her own during lockdown and I hoped flowers would cheer her up when she looked out of her window.

WHAT GARDENING ADVICE WOULD YOU LIKE TO SHARE?

I learnt to be careful not to plant too many things in one place. The lettuce seeds were so tiny, and I didn't realise quite how many I'd sown until millions of seedlings appeared. Give things enough room to grow. I only grew 6 tomato plants, but they turned into a massive jungle – you could hardly get to the tomatoes.

WHAT DID YOU DISCOVER THAT YOU WILL REPEAT?

It was really relaxing working in the soil and thinking about things while I did it. I will definitely try to have some sort of garden space when I am older, however small it is. It is so exciting to grow things from nothing and then to eat them.

WHAT PLANT WOULD YOU NOT BE WITHOUT IN YOUR GARDEN?

Beans. The beans went crazy and grew so much taller than I thought they would. I had to add string for them to climb so I could direct their growth up the wall. Even then they blocked out the sun from my peas and made picking very tricky. So next year I plant to remember to plant the tallest vegetables near the wall and the shortest ones near the path.

#newgardens

@swinglerlynsey

Name: Lynsey Swingler
Location: Eastbourne, Sussex, England

If you build it, they will come

Two new gardens were created with love

DESCRIBE YOUR GARDEN.
I want to tell you about two happy gardens. The first is my own – a family garden for myself, my husband, two teenagers, three chickens and a dog. It has two patios: one gets the sun in the morning, the other has the sun until the evening. We have a mixture of trees, shrubs, herbaceous perennials, fruit and veg. We have lots of raised beds, a chicken coup and a rather lovely brick path. The newest addition is the wildlife pond and the new border, where a frog has recently moved in. I'm happiest when a can hear the buzz of bees or see the birds feeding. Then I feel I've done a good job.

My second garden is the Ocklynge Rainbow Garden – a school vegetable and flower garden created this year. The soil from digging out my pond (so much soil), was used to fill 7 very colourful raised vegetable planters at school. The school garden was created on a shoe-string budget,

with donated pallets, old tyres and seeds rescued by a friend when they were being thrown out by the local supermarket.

The children of keyworkers used the beds to create a beautiful vegetable garden.

DO YOU GARDEN ALONE?
At home I do the gardening, and in school over lockdown I gardened with the children of key workers, aged 7-11.

WHAT WAS YOUR LOCKDOWN EXPERIENCE?
The children of key workers and some vulnerable children came into school throughout lockdown.

Although I'd always intended to get the Rainbow Garden up and running for this summer, it took on a special significance. It was brilliant to be able to have this bright, beautiful space where the children could learn to grow potatoes, tomatoes, carrots, beetroot, courgettes and peas. I was so lucky that I was able to garden at home and come into work and garden there too.

WHY HAS YOUR GARDEN BEEN SO IMPORTANT OVER LOCKDOWN?
At home I've created a pond and wildlife borders. I'm 47, but I was like a little kid when I saw our first frog, dragonflies and water beetles. If you build it, they will come! At school, the garden gave the children real moments of joy. They saw sunflowers get bigger than them. I've never seen peas create such happiness. Our home-grown jacket potatoes, cooked on the outdoor fire, were just brilliant.

WHAT IS YOUR FAVOURITE GARDENING HACK?
Pallet sleeves stacked on top of one another, lined and painted, make lovely raised beds. It makes access easier and reduces maintenance. In school, it also made it easier to organise the children and, for now, to stay socially distanced.

When laying a pond liner, sock feet are a must to avoid a puncture. The now mature pond has been a magnet for wildlife.

#newgardens

SHARE THE QUIRKIEST THING YOU'VE DONE IN YOUR GARDEN DURING LOCKDOWN?

At school we made butterfly feeders out of jam jars and string. We filled them with sugar water and decorated them. My daughter made her own set of hurdles out of garden canes when her athletics training was cancelled. A lot of string and glue were used.

ONE THING YOU DISCOVERED DURING LOCKDOWN?

Children will try veg they have grown themselves, if you cook it and eat it together. Well apart from beetroot! We're going to keep growing at school and extend our patch to include a chicken coop. We'll use the eggs for even more cooking.

WHAT PLANT WOULD YOU NOT BE WITHOUT?

Verbena bonariensis grows everywhere in my garden. It's wildlife friendly and just seems to blend other plants together. I love that it's so tall and airy.

> "Children will try veg they have grown themselves, if you cook it and eat it together. Well, apart from beetroot!"

WHAT (OR WHO) HAS BEEN YOUR MOST UNEXPECTED LOCKDOWN GARDEN VISITOR?

So many, but I was most thrilled when the frog turned up. I heard a plop as I walked by and there she was.

The Rainbow garden before and after - it's given so many people so much joy.

Growing hope

What my garden means to me

@jacquelinecurtis47

Name: Jacqueline Curtis
Location: Arundel, England

Although my energy levels have been low, I have been able to water and feed. As I nurtured the garden, it nurtured me. Like many gardeners I rarely just sit and look at my garden – but to recover I have been sitting and looking, and that has provided me with a better idea of what I do and don't like.

When lockdown eased, friends have been able to visit for socially distanced garden drinks and suppers. Most importantly of all, it allowed my family and grandchildren to visit.

"It's enabled me to sit and recuperate and although my energy levels have been low, I have been able to water and feed."

Nurtured by the garden

One week into lockdown I discovered I had breast cancer. Last autumn we had cleared the garden of standard topiary trees and a number of shrubs, all of which had outgrown their space. Spring 2020 was the time that replanting was to take place. Instead, I managed to order a number of perennial plants; a selection of salvias, perovskia (Russian sage), nepeta (cat mint) and ferns. I planted these the week before my operation, but they are not what I had originally planned. The garden does not feel particularly mine and is overly blue in colour due to my selection from what was available. But it was a start and it's enabled me to sit and recuperate.

#newgardens

The best investment during lockdown was a table tennis table - we have been having constant tournaments.

"I've taken to cooking onion bhaji's in the deep fat fryer in the garden - keeps the smell outside."

A year in the making

@circlesquaregd

Name: Carmel Dutton
Location: Ripon, North Yorkshire, England

#ornamentalgrasses #mygarden

DESCRIBE YOUR GARDEN.

We moved to our new build house in a village last year. The garden is much smaller than at any of our previous houses, but I think it's going to be our favourite. We have managed to incorporate so many different areas and elements in all three sides of the garden. There is a large seating area, brick raised beds, a lawn, a deep planted border, an area for a water bowl and many sculptures.

The main part of the garden has the most spectacular view over the fields and is baked in sun all day and every evening we can watch the sun disappear over the horizon. I've never had a garden before with so much sun, so it's allowed me to plant numerous sun-loving perennials, which have been bursting with colour all summer long.

The front of the house is in shade most of the day and I've managed to plant my much-loved tree fern there, along with lots of other ornamental grasses and ferns. The one big challenge our garden has is we are exposed to the wind. Mind you, the view is worth it!

DO YOU GARDEN ALONE?

My husband and I plant and maintain the garden. Next door's two-year old twin girls have helped me keep it watered!

WHAT WAS YOUR LOCKDOWN EXPERIENCE?

I have actually quietly enjoyed lockdown; I have loved having my family around me. In ordinary times, my husband would usually be away with work in London a couple of days a week, our eldest at university and our youngest out at work every day. All of sudden, all four of us were at home, working in different rooms but having every meal together. I know we were the lucky ones.

WHY WAS YOUR GARDEN SO IMPORTANT OVER LOCKDOWN?

North Yorkshire is beautiful but, like everyone else, our wings were clipped, and we were faced with only going out for essentials. At the same time, my elderly mother's health deteriorated quickly. The care home where she had lived for the past year were fantastic and allowed my sisters and I to be in a mini lockdown in her room over Easter weekend. She died on Easter Monday. Our garden then became our peace, our quiet – but also a reminder of new life. The new plants were growing so fast. The colour and the wildlife were so uplifting.

WHAT IS YOUR FAVOURITE GARDENING TIP?

My garden advice is to get yourself a Hori-Hori (Japanese weeding tool and knife), as Ann-Marie suggested. I had never even heard of them before. It's fantastic, what a brilliant tool, I love it.

SHARE THE QUIRKIEST THING YOU'VE DONE IN YOUR GARDEN DURING LOCKDOWN?

I bought my husband an outdoor table tennis table for his birthday on 23rd April and our 19-year-old son and him have had constant tournaments. Oh, and I've taken to cooking onion bhaji's in the deep fat fryer in the garden – keeps the smell outside!

WHAT IS THE ONE THING YOU DISCOVERED DURING LOCKDOWN THAT YOU WILL REPEAT?

Family meals around a table. So often we are all so busy, in and out. Lockdown has given us time to talk.

WHAT PLANT WOULD YOU NOT BE WITHOUT IN YOUR GARDEN?

A new find – *Ceanothus* 'Marie Simon'. I'd always thought ceanothus were blue but came across a pink one. It has flowered all summer long.

WHAT (OR WHO) HAS BEEN YOUR MOST UNEXPECTED LOCKDOWN GARDEN VISITOR?

We have a hedgehog visit. It does a route from next door across four gardens. We all message each other on the group chat to say it's on its way.

#newgardens

Before the new design was
implemented the garden was
just rough grass (bottom left).
Now it is unrecognisable.

"I begged and borrowed plants
from friends and family and
planted lots of seeds."

@ruthienoak

Name: Ruth Noak
Location: Walsall, England

#myrealgarden #englishgardens

I'm so happy with the result

The new garden created a connection with my older neighbours

DO YOU GARDEN ALONE?
I live alone, but during lockdown Betel UK came to bring my garden to life. This is a charity that uses its proceeds to support the homeless and those recovering from addiction.

WHAT WAS YOUR LOCKDOWN EXPERIENCE?
I entered lockdown without a job, and with seemingly little chance of finding one, after promising interviews were pulled. Lockdown didn't really change much for me as I'd built a routine of exercising and spending time outside every day. In March I was directing the Betel UK team to put my plan into action, which was pretty scary, but incredible to see it coming to life. My challenge was my impatience waiting for them to finish. I finally got to start planting at the beginning of May.

WHY WAS YOUR GARDEN SO IMPORTANT OVER LOCKDOWN?
Gardening has given me focus when I could have easily let the situation get me down. I've loved the stretch of learning new things, and the surprising discoveries along the way (I love orange flowers – quite a revelation!) It's also created connections between me and my older neighbours who are much more experienced gardeners, and who have frequently left trays of seedlings on my doorstep.

SHARE THE QUIRKIEST THING YOU'VE DONE IN YOUR GARDEN DURING LOCKDOWN?
In the middle of the heatwave, sitting in my garden with my cup of tea in the pouring rain, enjoying the beautiful sights, smells and sounds while cooling down.

WHAT IS THE ONE THING YOU DISCOVERED DURING LOCKDOWN THAT YOU WILL REPEAT?
Vegetable growing has been a revelation and a joy. Some I won't repeat, like curly kale (too many places for the caterpillars to hide). Others, such as courgettes, tomatoes, beans, peas and pumpkins, will become an annual tradition.

WHAT PLANT WOULD YOU NOT BE WITHOUT IN YOUR GARDEN?
This year it's been sunflowers – fantastic for covering my fences while I wait for plants to mature, and just generally for being miraculous at growing from such a small seed so quickly.

WHAT (OR WHO) HAS BEEN YOUR MOST UNEXPECTED LOCKDOWN GARDEN VISITOR?
I've had a fantastic variety of bees. My favourite is the leaf cutter bee. How they manage to wrap the leaf around them and still fly gracefully is amazing.

DESCRIBE YOUR GARDEN.
I have a small (7m x 16m) garden, which has been neglected since I moved in 6 years ago. I was already out of work prior to lockdown and had completed an online garden design course and redesigned my garden. Thinking I'd have a new job by then, the landscaping was planned for March 2020. Covid-19 meant this wasn't to be, but I went ahead anyway and had lots of quality time to plant my garden. Unfortunately, what I didn't have was a job to fund the planting! I begged and borrowed plants from friends and family and planted lots of seeds (inspired by @myrealgarden).

I'm so happy with the result, and everything I've learned along the way. Fortunately, I've since gained a job and I'm now planning the 'real' planting scheme.

The garden has been transformed from an overgrown mess of leylandii hedges, to an open space with lots of potential. It's packed full of vegetables and annual flowers. I've gone with the cottage garden vibe this year, and it has brought me much joy with new discoveries every day.

#newgardens

Growing hope

What my garden means to me

@loveyourgarden2.0

Name: Eve Kerrigan
Location: Lincolnshire, England

at Durham University who had no idea what path to take in the future. Now, I could not be more excited to pursue a career in horticulture once I have completed my degree and I've been inspired to enrol to study my RHS Level 2 qualification in the Principles of Horticulture.

On a more personal level, gardening has acted like an anchor, whereby the only thing that I could be certain of was that the garden would be constantly evolving and growing alongside me. This allowed me to put my trust in Mother Nature's hands and let her lead the way through my discovery of the joys of gardening and the stability and peace that it offers for a future career. I can't wait to see what the future holds for me.

> **"I could not be more excited to pursue a career in horticulture once I have completed my degree."**

Career change

Unlike many others in the UK, lockdown for my family was a very peaceful yet productive experience. The first half was spent making scrubs and surgical theatre hats for our local hospitals; in total, my family and I were able to make over 150 garments. The second half consisted of spending time outdoors, getting my fingers into gardening and learning about nature. I also completed my second year of university online, studied for assessments as a volunteer RNLI lifeboat crew member, and began an RHS qualification.

For me, gardening has been life changing during the lockdown period. I started this uncertain time as a second year Criminology student

Second revamp underway

@no30designstudio

Name: Sara Edwards
Location: Herefordshire, England

2 DAYS AGO

DESCRIBE YOUR GARDEN.
The garden has evolved many times since the house was built in 1968, as it's been in the family all that time; this is its second revamp under my tenure. The deck was the first major change we made when we took over the house. It looked down to a lawn curving through beds with mixed perennials and grasses, with a large Bramley apple tree dominating and a leaky pond hidden behind.

The bottom of the garden was cleared in the autumn of 2019 to make way for a large man cave, and the back of the garage was earmarked for my 'life goal' – a cedar greenhouse. It went up on the day after lockdown started, when I pretty much moved in!

Lockdown gave me time to prep the garden for the re-design. I dug up the whole garden, potting up any plants I want to re-use, clearing perennial weeds, ready for the new design to be implemented. The design is based around a circular lawn, pergola, sunken firepit and two new ponds. Planting will focus more on evergreen structure and foliage plants, with an exotic twist, and splashes of colour.

DO YOU GARDEN ALONE?
Our new design is a joint effort with the aim of it becoming our garden. I'm hoping to encourage my partner to spend more time in it and help look after it.

WHAT WAS YOUR LOCKDOWN EXPERIENCE?
The greenhouse really was my saviour. I have spent so much time sowing seeds, willing them to grow and learning how to take cuttings. I have had many successes and a lot of failures, but I have recorded them all in my greenhouse journal so I can learn from them next year, when I intend to continue sowing and growing.

WHY WAS YOUR GARDEN SO IMPORTANT OVER LOCKDOWN?
When lockdown happened, we decided to capitalise on the situation and set about taking out the leaking pond, an old concrete base and lots of rubbish. We filled an 8-yard skip from our efforts. It kept us busy and gave us something positive to look forward to. In the evenings we enjoyed eating and having a beer outside on the deck, grateful to have such a lovely outdoor space to relax in.

WHAT IS YOUR BEST MEMORY OF YOUR GARDEN?
It is hard to describe the feeling of joy that I felt on seeing my first seeds germinate. Then the joy is repeated when you share your plant babies with friends so they can enjoy nurturing them and update you on their progress.

#newgardens

Lockdown gave us time to lift all the plants to make way for the new look and my dream greenhouse. It was hard work but worth it.

WHAT IS YOUR FAVOURITE GARDENING TIP?

After taking lots of cuttings the conventional way, I learnt from the well-known expert Jimi Blake (Hunting Brook Gardens, Ireland) that if you put them in pure sand, don't trim back the top leaves and keep them well watered. My positive results proved that this is the way to go.

SHARE THE QUIRKIEST THING YOU'VE DONE IN YOUR GARDEN DURING LOCKDOWN?

In 1999, I buried our old dog Honey in the garden. Then, when we were digging out the soil for the greenhouse raised bed, guess what we dug up (and swiftly put back!)? Happily, everything planted in the 'Honey Pit' has thrived.

WHAT IS THE ONE THING YOU DISCOVERED DURING LOCKDOWN THAT YOU WILL REPEAT?

I have a long wish list of weird and wonderful plants that are not readily available, but that you can grow from seed. This year I have had a few successes and I intend trying to propagate more of my wish list each year.

WHAT (OR WHO) HAS BEEN YOUR MOST UNEXPECTED LOCKDOWN GARDEN VISITOR?

I have a resident frog in the greenhouse, who doesn't like getting splashed when I am watering. My partner thinks we need to put in a mini pond for him.

YOUR GREATEST GARDENING SUCCESS DURING LOCKDOWN?

My mystery tomato plants, grown from seed saved from ones grown last year. I failed to write down their name. They are triffid-like, a cordon variety with brownish coloured fruit... answers on a postcard?

"My cedar greenhouse went up on the day after lockdown started, and I pretty much moved in!"

212

#newgardens

@gardening.is.life

Allocate a day of the week for feeding – Feeding Friday has given me great results.
Sally Hart
@harts.and.flowers

Petra Sturgeon
Be brave and follow your heart. All time in the garden is time well spent, even if you make mistakes. I find it's not just the garden that is growing – I am too.

Hacks, Tips & Tricks

A blank canvas or a radical revamp – discover some great ideas for your new patch of paradise

Tie a strip of brightly coloured cloth or ribbon through the handles of your fork, trowel, and Hori Hori knife and you'll never spend hours searching for them in full flower borders again.
Ruth Thomas @grannylondon

Get stuck in. I have dug out about three tonnes of rubble by hand over lockdown and even unearthed some false teeth! I live in a terrace, so anything that comes in or out of the garden has to go through the house. If we can dot it, you can too!
Anni Peckham
@thisgreencity

My top tip for thriving plants? Focus on soil first, every time.
Therese Lang
@thereselangscape

Watching your garden evolve really is so rewarding, and is definitely worth all the scratched legs and broken nails!
Ellie Luk
@gascon_gardener

@jackykip

Jacky Kippenberger
You can move plants around the garden in spring and autumn if you carefully lift them with lots of soil and keep them well watered.

Growing hope

What our gardens mean to us

@tram_cat

Name: Kate Main
Location: Edinburgh, Scotland

for me. Finding the @myrealgarden community on Instagram has also given me, as a solo gardener, my first gardening community.

> **"What a luxury it was just to be able to go outside during those sunny early months."**

Creating distraction and community

My mum had a huge stroke on Hogmanay (31st December 2019) and was in hospital until about a week before lockdown in March 2020. We were able to get her into a nursing home but then we weren't allowed to visit her from the start of lockdown until July. That was tough, even though the rest of my family stayed healthy. Bringing my garden back from its slightly neglected state and having the time and space to work outside has been so important. I appreciate what a luxury it was just to be able to go outside during those sunny early months. I'm not a creative or artistic person but gardening fills that space

"I enjoyed the camaraderie of new online friends and local plant swappers."
Carrie Leyland
@carrieleyland

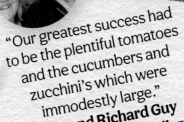

"Our greatest success had to be the plentiful tomatoes and the cucumbers and zucchini's which were immodestly large."
Mary and Richard Guy
@maryguy6 @richardkguy

"I live and garden alone, but I love welcoming friends and family to my little patch."
Marie Irvine @swottybotty

Sunny thoughts

"Growing some plants and vegetables for the first time rather than just buying them has been hugely satisfying."
Sarah Rush
@sarah.rush40

"This garden has been my first real opportunity to show my character and what I have learned over the years."
Panda Sheridan
@pandacoates

"I garden with my husband Nick and my mini schnauzer Lola who likes to supervise in between us throwing a tennis ball."
Jason Bishop
@wannabe_gardener_gsy

"I definitely let off steam by gardening. My husband can usually tell if I have not had a chance to spend time with my hands in the soil!"
Lucy Parker
@lucyparker45

"A firm memory is lying on the sun lounger with a beer listening to the goldfinches."
Daisy Hayden
@thepengegardener

Our supporters

Our grateful thanks to all those who have pre-ordered or supported our book

Elise Prosser
Adrienne Bamford
Agnes Hackett
Ailsa Burton
Alex Cullen
Alex Denman
Alison Renyard
Alitex
Amanda Gibson
Amanda Stothert
Ami Marshall
Amy Murray
Andy Sturgeon
Angela Ridge
Angie Boakes
Ann Brodie
Ann lee
Anna Edwards
Anna Karlsson
Anne Francis
Anne Morgan
Anni Peckham
Annie Wright
Angela Arnold
Barbara Spencer
Barry and Vanessa De
Morgan
Becca Morgan
Becca Smith
Ben laing
Beverley Setchell
Branka Poklecki
Bridget Galloway
Camilla Swift
Carmel Dutton
Caroline Burvill
Caroline Graham

Caroline Hill
Caroline Shenton
Carolyn Foster
Carolyn Ramsamy
Cat Woolfe
Catherine Gilpin
Catherine Woodham
Catriona Barclay
Charlotte Cummins
Charlotte Lorimer
Charlotte Tomalin
Christine Casagrande
Christine Sennett
Christine Smith
Christopher Woodward
Claire Vennis
Claire Ling
Clare Anderson
Clare Andrews
David McIntosh
Dawn Evans
Dean Halsey
Debbie Mitchell
Donna Loveday
Eileen Mills
Elaine Portch
Elaine Tier-Quick
Eliza Gray
Ellie Luk
Emily Crowley-Wroe
Emma Seddon
Erica James
Eveline Aregger
Fia Selmer
Fiona Jones
Fiona Pruden
Gaze Burvill

Giles Heap
Gill Bolton
Gill Brookes
Gillian Davies
Gillian Kelly
Heather Anderson
Helen Fickling
Helen Millard
Hilary-Fay Mellor
Hywel Jones
Iain Davies
Ian Martin
Ilse Vanoosterhout
Jackie Peck
Jackie Sippitt
Jackie Weavers
Jacky Kippenberger
Jacqui Fox
Jacqui Garrard
Jacquie Cox
Jain Keenan-Livingstone
Jake Catling
James Alexander-Sinclair
Jan Crouch
Jane Jefferies
Janeen Woodward
Jason Bishop
Jayne Davidson
Jenny Crane
Jessica Warman
Jo Gallonn
Jo Thompson
Jo Hopkins
Joan Wright
Joanne Gallon
Jonty Joyce
Julia Paul

Julie Facey
Julie Garriock
Julie Giles
Justine Fraser
Karen Judge
Karen Stark
Karen Wildgoose
Kat Kinch
Kate Ebbens
Kate Main
Kate McGorty
Katherine Richardson
Katie Patton
Kerry Connolly
Kevin Gilbert
Kim Dalton
Krissie Sorel-Cameron
Laura Willcox
Leila Sherratt
Lesley Cook
Lesley Spicer
Lia Leendertz
Linda Byron
Linda Pearce
Lisa Camlin
Lisa Downing
Lisa Wilkinson
Liz Cooper
Liz Daniels
Liz Meyer
Liz Rentzsch
Liz Templer
Location Landscapes Ltd
Louise Farara
Louise French
Louise Furber
Lucy Allen

Lucy Parker
Luned Fortt
Lynda Griffiths
Lynn Shaw
Lynsey Swingler
Maarit Lilley
Mags Gilroy
Mandy Balcombe
Mandy Bradshaw
Mar Fernández
Marcella Argue
Marcelle Stewart
Margery Fawcett
Marie-Louise Agius
Marion Keogh
Mary Bulgin
Mary Spurr
Mary Guinness
Mary Guy
Mary Whelan
Matt Keightley
Maximo Cabeza
Melanie Edge
Melanie Farrow
Michael Palmer
Michelle Corbett
Michelle Moon
Mieke Philips
Mugs Gohl
Nel Logan
Nelly Hall
Nichola Henson
Nicola McGinty
Osmawani Osman
Petra Sturgeon
Patricia Calcraft
Paul Fraser

Paula White
Pauline Chapman
Pauline Smith
Pauline Walley
Perry Rachel
Peter Aylett
Philippa McCullough
Philippa Williams
Piotr Ashwin-Siejkowski
Piper Hocking
Rachel Hipperson
Rachel McLeod
Ray Couplan
Rebecca Evans
Rebecca Richards
Richard Guy
Richard Jackson
Ricki Hale
Robert Jones
Rosalind Robertson
Rosalind Vincent
Rosaline Nutsugah
Rosemary Nabarro
Ruth Thomas
Sally Hart
Sam Phillips
Sara Edwards
Sarah Clayton
Sarah McMurray
Sarah Phillipps
Sarah Rush

Sarah Waddington
Scott Spencer
Sevin Harkess
Shane Eason
Sharon Harrison
Sharon Welch
Sheila Coolbear
Sheila Goggs
Shona Moth
Shweta Mehta
Simon Botherway
Sophie van Gerwen
Stacey McGovern
Stephen Lacey
Sue Hewison
Sue Hubbard
Sue Townsend
Sue Vincent

Sue Wheeler
Sue Wood
Susan Freeborn
Susan Imiolek
Susan Read
Susan Wright
Susanne Baker
Susie Warwick
Sylke Jakob
Tracey Todd
Trish Hill
Teresa Byington
Teresa Chaplow
The Garden Design Co Ltd
Tim Howell
Tina Lovesey
Tracey O'Conner
Treeza Sodah
Victoria Crumby
Warren Haskins
Yukie Hanada

 C A N D I D E We would like to give a special call-out to our very first backer, Candide, the fabulous plant and gardening platform, who had such faith in our mission that they supported us before we even had a page to share. Whether you are a beginner or expert, Candide is an indispensable tool which helps you identify, buy and care for plants as well as buy tickets to some of our most treasured gardens. Do check out their website **candidegardening.com** or just download the app. You'll wonder how you ever gardened without it!

greenfingers charity
creating magical gardens
for children in hospices

We are thrilled that your backing for this book means that we are able to donate some
of the proceeds from our first print run to a wonderful UK charity, Greenfingers.

Greenfingers Charity has a truly worthwhile mission to support life-limited children, and their families,
who spend time in children's hospices by creating inspiring gardens for them to relax in and enjoy.
These beautiful, well-designed spaces offer children an opportunity to embrace the benefits
of being in the fresh air and experience the natural environment.

As garden lovers we are sure all our readers will appreciate just how precious this shared outdoor time is.
Here is their website address if you would like to learn more about the work of Greenfingers Charity or find out
how you can support their great cause: **www.greenfingerscharity.org.uk**